INSIGHT COMPACT GUIDES

D

Compact Guide: Denmark is the ideal quick-reference guide to the land of the Vikings. It tells you all you need to know about the country's many attractions, from the beaches of the Baltic to the cliffs of Møn, from the Little Mermaid in Copenhagen to the birthplace of Hans Christian Andersen.

This is one of almost 100 titles in *Insight Guides'* series of pocket-sized, easy-to-use guidebooks intended for the independent-minded traveller. *Compact Guides* are in essence travel encyclopedias in miniature, designed to be comprehensive yet portable, as well as up-to-date and authoritative.

Star Attractions

An instant reference to some of Denmark's most popular tourist attractions to help you on your way.

Town Hall Square, Copenhagen p19

National Museum, Copenhagen p20

Nyhavn Waterfront, Copenhagen p23

Ribe Cathedral p29

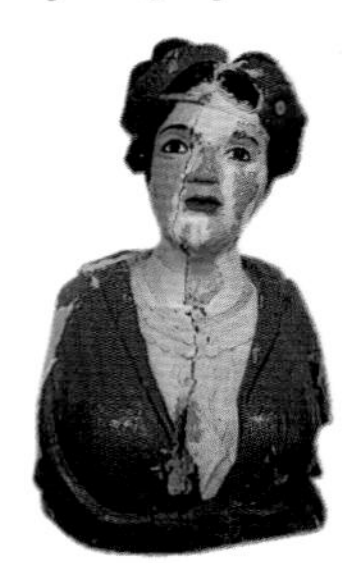

Strandungsmuseum St George p31

Legoland p51

H C Andersen's birthplace p63

Trelleborg Viking Fort p68

Church of Our Lady, Kalundborg p74

Chalk cliffs of Møn, p74

Bornholm Island, p77

DENMARK

Introduction

Places

Culture

Leisure

Practical Information

Denmark – Land of Contrasts

Opposite: Copenhagen's Little Mermaid

Seemingly endless beaches, backed by a huge belt of sand-dunes where summer holiday homes cluster together out of the wind: this is the Denmark that greets most visitors, for the North Sea coast of Jutland is by far the most popular holiday destination in the country.

But Denmark has much more to offer than most people think. It comprises 407 islands, all of which have names, and almost 100 of which are inhabited; no part of the mainland is further than 52km (32 miles) from the sea. Indeed, Denmark would be a country made up entirely of islands if the large peninsula of Jutland were not attached to northern Germany. Denmark's 67-km (41-mile) border with Germany pales in comparison with its 7,500km (4,660 miles) of coastline: the mud-flats and dyked marshland in southern Jutland, the level coastline of western Jutland with its lagoons and sand bars, the fjords cutting deep into the mainland, the sounds from eastern Jutland to Sjælland, a set of 'Caribbean' islands off southern Fyn, chalk cliffs on Møn and in eastern Sjælland, and rocky coasts with Mediterranean flair and the best beaches in Europe around Bornholm.

Cliffs of Møn

Denmark's longest river (158km/98 miles), the Gudenå, winds its way across central Jutland. It connects with some of the finest lakes in the country, situated in the thickly-wooded area near Silkeborg.

Denmark is a lot more versatile than its geographical statistics (highest elevation: 174m/570ft) suggest. Its many low hills were formed during the last Ice Age. Later, the forests and moors developed. But the landscape has been most markedly changed by the hand of man: meadows and fields full of rape dotted with the occasional farmstead or village nestling round its whitewashed church, are a typical sight. Such small villages are more than worth a visit, many of them successfully combining their half-timbered charms with all the requirements of modern living. Indeed, the amount of good modern architecture and art to be seen in the streets, squares and museums of Denmark's provincial towns more than stands up to international comparison.

Typical village house

The small number of major towns and the busy metropolis of Copenhagen compete with one another with their excellent museums and cultural events both traditional and modern – in fact, there's always something to suit a wide range of tastes.

The People

The Danes have a reputation for being relaxed, cheerful, keen on beer, sociable and generous; among Scandinavians they are considered the southerners of the north, con-

Ladies still smoke cigars

Flying the flag

tent to turn a blind eye. These are just generalisations, of course, because a population of 5.2 million in today's Europe can't be so easily pigeon-holed. The Danish character is as varied as the country itself: rooted in the soil, it is often reticent in the more rural areas, and can be wilful, even eccentric, on the islands.

In the cities, on the other hand, people are generally much more broad-minded, and may even be described as noisy and raucous on occasions. The popular image of ladies smoking cigars in dimly-lit pubs still holds, of course, but in the towns you will also find young women dressed in the very latest fashions sipping cappuccinos outside French-style cafés.

A lot of visitors soon learn to value that special Danish version of *gemütlichkeit* known as *hygge*. It should be mentioned here that the borderline between 'public' and 'private' is nowhere else in Europe as hazy as it is in Denmark – here, people feel at home everywhere. What is more, there is a healthy mixture of respect for tradition and a marked tolerance towards others. Danish everyday life is noticeably relaxed: words like 'hurry', 'hectic' and 'stress' are alien concepts here.

Indeed, opinion polls have proved that the Danes feel more at home in their own country than any other nation in the world. Their national pride – everywhere in evidence, usually in the form of red-and-white flags fluttering at every turn – is far more gentle than aggressive. The preservation of Danish culture is a high priority in both private and public life. The 700 or so official museums of history, art and folklore – a huge number for such a small country – are more than proof of this.

Proud to be Danish

Administration

Denmark has a population of about 5.2 million. Each of the 43,000sq m (462,843sq ft) of Denmark is occupied by an average of 120 Danes, and the country is divided into 14 administrative areas, known as counties, and two independent cities, or communes. Around one-quarter of the population lives either in or very close to the capital, Copenhagen.

This puts the island of Sjælland ahead as far as statistics are concerned: 17 percent of the country's surface area is inhabited by more than 40 percent of the entire Danish population (ie roughly 300 people per sq km). Lolland and Falster and 46 smaller islands also belong to the county of Storstrøm, and have a combined population of roughly 117,000. Bornholm is actually a county in its own right, covering an area of 588sq km (227sq miles) and with a population of 45,000. Fyn and 99 islands – almost 20 of which are inhabited – form an independent county 3,486sq km (1,346sq miles) in size and with approximately 500,000 inhabitants. The Jutland peninsula – which includes 130 uninhabited islands and 23 inhabited – has a surface area of nearly 30,000sq km (11,580sq miles), and comprises seven counties with a combined population of almost 2.4 million. This part of the country also contains Denmark's most thinly-populated county: Ringkøbing (55 inhabitants per sq km).

Carved altarpiece

Religion

Every ninth Dane is a member of the Evangelical Lutheran *Folkekirche*, the country's official church. There are also around 140,000 adherents of other faiths, including roughly 60,000 Muslims and almost 30,000 Catholics; the latter have 88 churches.

The Nykirke on Bornholm

Language

The Danish language is Nordic, and a subdivision of the Germanic group. Although their languages are related, Scandinavians still have quite a few difficulties in communicating with one another; Danes and Norwegians have the fewest problems, because one of Norway's two official languages derives from the Danish spoken when it formed part of Denmark-Norway (until 1814). Danish also has several affinities with German.

Danish has several special letters: æ/ø/å. Pronunciation in general is quite complicated. A lot of letters change their pronunciation when combined with others, and several letters are 'unvoiced'. The special letters aren't too difficult to pronounce, though: æ – e as in *pear*; ø – u as in *fur*; and å –aw as in *paw*.

The grammar is simple, apart from the irregular verbs. Danish has only two genders, like French. Articles (*en* and

The Velje Museum of Art concentrates on graphics

et, and in the plural *ne*) go in front of the noun if indefinite, and after it if definite, ie a house = *et hus*, the house = *huset*, houses = *huse*, the houses = *husene*.

Climate

Don't forget the sun lotion

Denmark is situated in the temperate zone at the meeting point of several air masses, and the climate can be very changeable, especially in western Jutland. Brisk winds – mostly westerly – are typical, though they tend to die down towards evening. Despite the low elevation, there are noticeable differences in precipitation between the west (average), centre (high) and east (low) parts of the country; this effect can also be seen in miniature on larger islands, especially Bornholm.

Economy

Since 1945 Denmark has changed from a predominantly agrarian land into a modern industrial state, and has become an exporter of raw materials. The cause of such change is the systematic prospecting beneath the North Sea. Important exports alongside oil and gas include medicine, food and beverages, and also furniture. Danish firms are also among the world's leading producers of windmill farm technology.

Denmark's main trading partners, in order of importance, are Germany, Sweden and Great Britain.

Agriculture, forestry and fishing are the three traditionally important branches of the economy, taking up a full 25 percent of the country's exports, but these industries are currently going through a crisis: only 5 percent of the total national workforce is employed in these sectors, and just 27 percent in industry. Most of the jobs available are in the service sector, and nearly 100,000 of them are in the tourist business alone.

Legoland

Most firms in Denmark are small or medium-sized, and there are hardly any large corporations. Internationally famous concerns that developed in Denmark include LEGO (toys), Carlsberg and Tuborg (beer), Bang & Olufsen (hifi and TV), Danfoss (installation technology) and Rockwool (insulation material). The white, seven-pointed star on a blue background, frequently seen on oil platforms, ships, containers and aeroplanes all over the globe, is the symbol of Maersk, the largest private shipping company in the world.

The high unemployment figure of around 10 percent has to be seen in relation to the high percentage, in international terms, of workforce available. Women's equality, for example, is really put into practice here: there are roughly as many working women as men. Denmark's large network of well-organised crèches means that mothers can work while their children are cared for.

Financial support for the unemployed, retraining and job creation schemes all form part of a protective social net. A model of its type in Europe since the 1960s and 1970s, the welfare system has now become a heavy financial burden and has recently faced cutbacks in several areas, despite increases in taxation. The tax rate of over 50 percent may seem high in international terms, but should be seen in relation to what it actually provides: medical insurance coverage, an old age pension, and also subsidies for a wide spectrum of cultural events both in the capital and in the provinces.

Carlsberg Brewery

A peaceful retirement

Politics and Government

Denmark is a hereditary constitutional monarchy. A popular constitution has been in force since 1849, though it was significantly amended in 1915 and again in1953. The 175 Danish members of the one-chamber parliament known as the *Folketing* are elected according to a complicated system of proportional representation. Each time a new *Folketing* is elected, Greenlanders and Faeroe Islanders are also entitled to vote, supplying two members of parliament each.

The last time any party gained an absolute majority was at the beginning of the 20th century; and even majority governments are a rarity. Ever since 1973, when the number of small parties in the *Folketing* went up to an average of 10, the proportions have been very fluid – there has not been a majority coalition for 20 years. New elections generally take place every two years or so; hardly any government ever manages to survive the full legislative period of four years.

The head of state since 1972 has been the country's popular queen, Margrethe II (born in 1940). She studied law and political science at universities in Denmark, France

Queen Margrethe

and England, and is fond of archaeology (she has taken part in excavations both at home and abroad); she is fluent in several languages (and has done some respected translations from French and Swedish) and is also a highly-respected artist. Although her function under the terms of the constitution is purely representative, Margrethe II continues to take a clear stand on several issues, particularly those involving social problems.

The queen is the official chief executive of the State Council and appends her signature to all laws that are passed. Whenever a new government is elected she has to ask one of the country's political leaders to work out a majority and, if possible, form a government. No minister can remain in office if the *Folketing* passes a vote of no confidence in him.

Denmark has shown a lot of global responsibility in recent years: it contributes a great deal to international aid, and Danish troops make up a large percentage of the UN forces sent to the world's crisis regions. Denmark is a member of NATO and of the EU.

As alliance partners, the Danish are considered reliable but also critical: no other country seems to be so efficient at implementing EU directives on the one hand while being so uninterested in community cooperation on the other *(see page 13)*. The Danes tend to worry about losing their special identity and their cultural independence in the European Union.

Greenland and the Faeroe Islands

As a relic of its colonial past, the kingdom of Denmark also embraces two islands in the North Atlantic which are not described in any further detail in this guide: **The Faeroe Islands** (1,399sq km/540sq miles; pop. 45,000) and **Greenland** (2,175,600sq km/840,005sq miles, 85 percent of which is covered by ice; pop. 55,000, comprising 85 percent Inuit and 15 percent of Danish descent). They each enjoy partial autonomy and have their own internationally acknowledged flags, coats-of-arms, car number-plates, etc, as well as their own parliaments and prime ministers.

The head of state of both countries is Queen Margrethe. The right of self-administration (granted to the Faeroes in 1948 and to Greenland in 1979) also extends to all internal affairs, though Copenhagen has the main say in foreign and defence policy matters. Both countries have their own postage stamps and the Faeroe islanders also have their own currency (Faeroese *krone*, equivalent to Danish *krone*) which can be used throughout the kingdom. Danish taxpayers support the budgets of both countries very generously (around 45 percent of all state income in Greenland, and 25 percent on the Faeroes).

Historical Highlights

20000BC The first signs of human habitation (worked flints).

3500–1800BC Stone Age. Megalithic tombs and dolmens still survive.

1800–500BC Bronze Age. Many burial mounds in evidence.

500BC–AD793 Iron Age, divided into a Celtic (500–0), Roman (0–400) and Germanic phase (400–800). Several human sacrifices take place in Jutland around AD400. The bodies, thrown into the moor, have remained preserved. First trading centres spring up in Ribe, in Haitabu near Schleswig and on the east coast of Fyn. Border fortifications in the south (Danevirke).

AD793 The plundering of the monastery of Lindisfarne in the northeast of England marks the beginning of the Viking Age. Attacks along the English and Frankish coasts follow, and extend as far as the Mediterranean and along the major rivers into Central Europe. Large numbers of Norsemen settle eastern England and the coast of northern France (Normandy). Vikings leave western Norway on major trips of discovery and settlement, reaching the Faeroe Islands, Iceland, Greenland and North America.

826 The monk Ansgar leads the attempt at converting the North, and the first churches are built around the middle of the 9th century.

c950 Centre of power moves to Jelling. Gorm becomes king of Jutland. He is succeeded by his son, Harald Bluetooth.

985–1014 Sweyn Forkbeard conquers England.

1018 Knud (Canute) the Great unites eastern England and parts of Norway under the Danish crown.

1035 After Knud's death the first Danish Empire collapses, and the Viking Age ends.

1074–1154 Royal power weakened by squabbles over succession. This strengthens the power of the church. Denmark receives its own archbishopric in 1104.

1154–82 Knud's son Valdemar the Great restores the kingship. Denmark expands as far as the Baltic. Copenhagen is founded in 1167 by Absalon, bishop of Roskilde.

1240–1340 A period of decline that began under Valdemar Sejr (1202–41) continues with the rise to power in the Baltic of the Hanse. By 1300, Denmark is bankrupt and deeply in debt to the Holstein nobility. For eight years (1332–40) Denmark has no king, and is ruled by the counts of Holstein.

1340–75 Valdemar IV Atterdag unites the country and restores the throne.

1375–1412 Margaret I, daughter of Valdemar Atterdag and wife of the Norwegian king Haakon VI, becomes regent of Denmark in 1375, and in 1380 of Norway (including Faeroe Islands, Iceland and Greenland) and also Sweden. She is never actually crowned. In 1397 her adoptive son Erik VII of Pomerania becomes king of the three Nordic kingdoms in an official ceremony in Kalmar (the 'Kalmar Union'), but Margaret continues to be influential until her death in 1412.

1412–39 Erik VII makes Copenhagen his capital in 1417 and has a palace built in Helsingør. From 1425 onwards all ships using the Sound have to pay a toll; though profitable, this results in centuries-long arguments with other powers.

1520 The execution of 80 Swedish nobles in Stockholm on the orders of Christian II (the 'Stockholm Bloodbath') fails to halt the dissolution of the Kalmar Union.

1523–34 Gustav Vasa's coronation as king of Sweden spells the end of the Kalmar Union, though Norway still remains part of Denmark. Christian II is deposed. The ensuing civil war ends in the defeat of the burghers and farmers by the nobility. In 1534 Christian III is crowned and tries to make the throne hereditary. A Danish Lutheran church is sanctioned.

1534–96 The nobility prospers, apart from a brief war against Sweden (1563–70). Around 1500 Renaissance manor houses and castles are built in Denmark, many of them on Fyn and Sjælland as well as eastern Jutland.

1596–1648 Many Renaissance buildings appear during the reign of Christian IV. His attempts to elevate Denmark to the status of a great power end in disaster, however: Sweden gains much Danish land. By the time of his death in 1648 Denmark is ruined.

1648–70 Frederick III plunges the country into a war with Sweden once again. Skåne and Blekinge (today Sweden's southern provinces) are lost, as is Bornholm for a while. Denmark loses a full third of its territory. Despite these defeats, in 1660 Frederick still manages to assert the power of the nobility and introduce absolutism.

1675–9 and 1700–20 Renewed wars with Sweden; then a period of peace until 1801.

1721 Hans Egede's trip to convert Greenland to Christianity puts the country under Danish influence once more.

1733 Danish peasants are forced by landlords to rent farms, or face conscription. Denmark acquires colonies in West Africa and the Caribbean, and participates in the slave trade.

1768–72 Johann Struensee, a German doctor, wins the trust of the half-mad king Christian VII and shares the bed of his 18-year-old queen. Struensee rules the country indirectly in this manner for almost 16 months before being hung, drawn and quartered in 1772.

1784 Crown Prince Frederick takes over as regent (becoming King Frederick VI from 1808). His adviser, CD Reventlow, introduced exemplary land reforms. Some 60 percent of the Danish peasants became landowners.

1801 During the Napoleonic Wars, an English fleet under Nelson destroys much of the Danish fleet in Copenhagen harbour, thus forcing Denmark to renounce the armed neutrality treaty of 1794 which it had entered into with Sweden, Russia and Prussia.

1807 English ships appear off Copenhagen again and demand the surrender of the Danish fleet. This happens after much of Copenhagen has been destroyed in a bombardment. After this, the Danes join the continental alliance against England, and suffer further defeats. By 1813 the land is bankrupt.

1814 The victorious powers dissolve the Denmark-Norway double monarchy at the Treaty of Kiel. Norway is ceded to Sweden, Helgoland to England, and Denmark is allowed to keep Iceland, the Faeroe Islands and Greenland. Despite all this, Denmark becomes the first country in Europe to introduce compulsory school education for all.

1814–48 The impoverished country experiences a cultural golden age. In 1843 the Tivoli Gardens are opened. In 1847, the first rail link is built between Roskilde and Copenhagen.

1848 Absolutism ends without a shot being fired. Frederick VII promises a new constitution, and signs it in 1849.

1848–50 First war fought over the Schleswig-Holstein question. It achieves nothing. The 'democratic' Danish king continues to reign as 'absolute' duke of Schleswig and Holstein, whose inhabitants feel more drawn to Germany.

1857 The toll for use of the Sound is abolished.

1864 Newly-crowned Christian IX signs a law passed by the democratically-elected parliament which confers the Danish constitution upon Schleswig but not Holstein. This results in a war against the German Confederation (Prussia and Austria) which ends in the Danish defeat at Dybbøl and the occupation of the whole of Jutland. Schleswig and Holstein now come under the control of Prussia and Austria, and the border runs along the Kongeå and to the south of Ribe and Kolding. Ærø also remains Danish.

1864–1914 EM Dalgas turns much of the land on Jutland into arable farmland. An industrial proletariat forms in the towns, resulting in a workers' movement and eventually in social democracy (first mandate in the Folketing in 1881). From 1882 onwards the cooperative movement wins ground in rural areas, forming the basis for the country's important agricultural export industry. Trade unions and employers' federations spread nationwide by 1890.

1914–18 Denmark remains neutral during World War I.

1915 Far-reaching constitutional reform. Women given the right to vote.

1917 Denmark's West Indian colonies (the Virgin Islands) sold to USA.

1920 A plebiscite held in Schleswig decides the boundary between Germany and Denmark, which is still in force today. Minorities remain on either side of it.

1924 First 'workers' government' under the leadership of the Social Democrats.

1935–40 Large construction programme is introduced to combat unemployment (University of Århus, Storstrøms Bridge, Little Belt Bridge).

1940–5 Though wishing to remain neutral in World War II, as it had in 1914–18, Denmark is invaded by the German army on 9 April 1940. Until 1943 the Germans keep their promise not to interfere in Danish internal affairs, and the country is even allowed to retain its own army. This period of cooperation comes to an end in 1943 when the government resigns. Denmark is recognised as one of the Allies. In October 1943 almost the whole of Denmark's Jewish population manages to escape across the Sound to Sweden, narrowly avoiding deportation. An underground war develops between the Danish Resistance on the one hand and the Germans and their collaborators on the other, and results in many executions and acts of sabotage.

1944 On 17 June Iceland, occupied by the Allies and partly independent since 1918, proclaims itself a republic against Danish wishes and receives full sovereignty.

1945 All of Denmark, apart from Bornholm, is liberated by the English on 5 May. On Bornholm the Germans hold out stubbornly for another four days, and Rønne and Neksø become the only Danish towns to endure aerial bombardment. The Red Army lands on Bornholm and stays there until March 1946.

1948 The Faeroe Islands are granted partial autonomy (*see page 10*).

1950–70 Modern satellite towns spring up around Copenhagen, and today roughly a quarter of Denmark's entire population lives in or near the capital (*see page 18*). Denmark and Sweden develop model welfare-state systems.

1953 A further constitutional revision includes provision for female succession to the Danish throne.

1955 The 'Bonn-Copenhagen Declaration' guarantees cultural preservation for the minorities who have been living on either side of the Danish-German border since it was drawn in 1920.

1972 Margrethe is crowned Queen Margrethe II of Denmark following the death of Frederick IX, who was born in 1899.

1973 Denmark joins the EC along with Great Britain and Ireland. However, plebiscites are necessary every step of the way towards a united Europe, because the Folketing cannot surrender any sovereignty without a 5–6 majority. (Plebiscites held in 1986, 1992 and 1993.)

1979 Parliament grants Greenland a limited amount of autonomy with regard to internal affairs (*see page 10*).

1986 Danes vote for closer European cooperation by a very slender margin.

1992 Danes say 'no' to the EU's Maastricht Treaty on economic and political union, but one year later vote 'yes' to the amended version of the Treaty.

1993 Prime minister Schlüter leaves office in disgrace after 10 years in power, accused of lying about measures to prevent Tamil refugees from entering the country from Sri Lanka. Thus ends 10 years of Conservative-Liberal rule. While out digging in a field in Dystrup, Djursland, two boys discover eight well-preserved bronze swords dating from 1600BC (Early Bronze Age). The astonishing discovery is hailed as one of the archaeological finds of the 20th century.

1998 As final agreement is reached on European Monetary Union, Denmark, together with the UK, decides not to enter the first wave. But the Danes do decide to endorse the the European Union's Amsterdam Treaty.

The 18-km (11-mile) long Great Belt Fixed Link, a combined bridge and tunnel link between Fyn and Sjæland, is completed. Work progressing on the Øresund Fixed Link between Copenhagen and southern Sweden.

HAVFRUEN

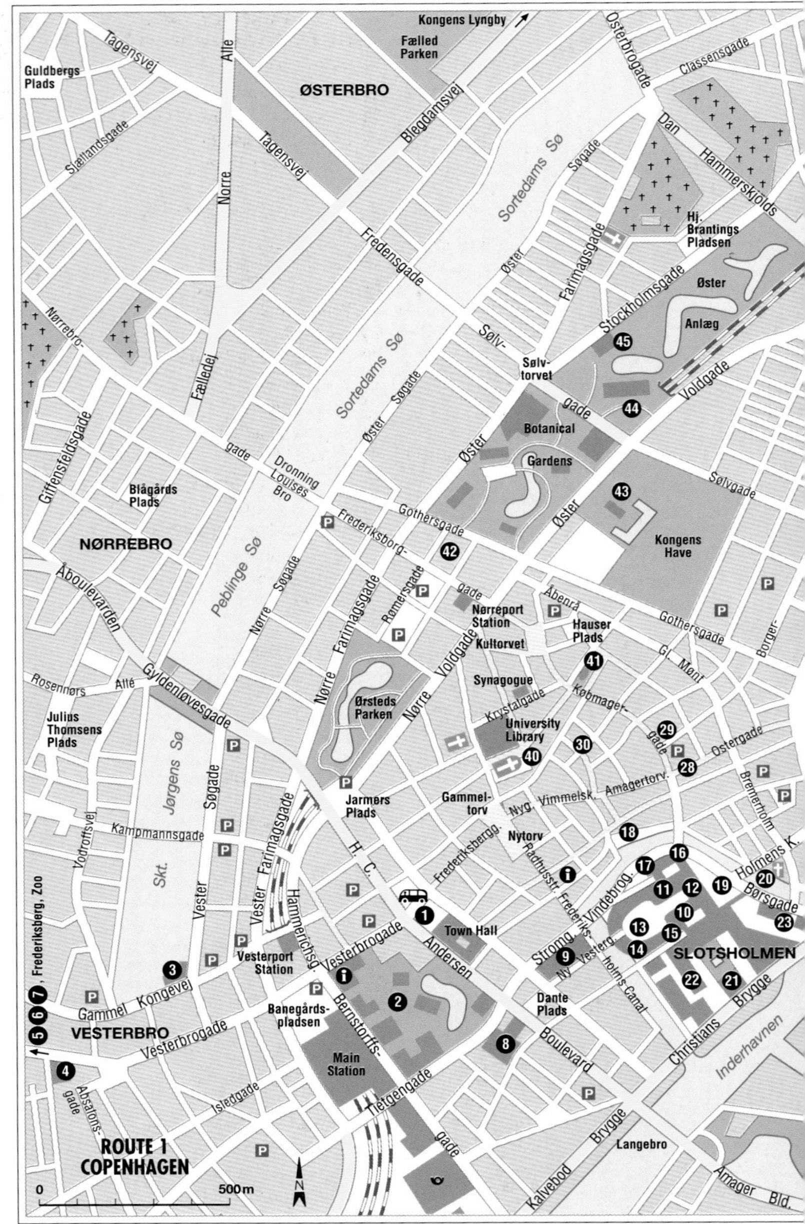

Kongens Lyngby
Fælled Parken
ØSTERBRO
Østerbrogade
Classensgade
Tagensvej
Guldbergs Plads
Nørre Allé
Sjællandsgade
Bledgamsvej
Sortedams Sø
Søgade
Dan Hammerskjölds
Hj. Brantings Pladsen
Fredensgade
Øster Farimagsgade
Stockholmsgade
Øster Anlæg
Nørrebro-
Fælledej
Sølv-
Sølvtorvet
Voldgade
Øster Søgade
gade
Botanical Gardens
Giffensfeldsgade
Dronning Louises Bro
Sølvgade
Blågårds Plads
Gothersgade
NØRREBRO
Frederiksborg-
Kongens Have
Åboulevarden
Peblinge Sø
Nørre Søgade
Nørre Farimagsgade
Rømersgade
Nørreport Station
Åbenrå
Hauser Plads
Kultorvet
Borger-
Rosennørs Allé
Gyldenløvesgade
Nørre Voldgade
Synagogue
Gl. Mønt
Krystalgade
Købmager-gade
Julius Thomsens Plads
Ørsteds Parken
University Library
Østergade
Jørgens Sø
Søgade
Jarmers Plads
Gammeltorv
Nyg.
Vimmelsk.
Amagertorv.
Bremerholm
Vodroffsvej
Kampmannsgade
Nytorv
Frederiksberg.
Radhusstr.
Holmens K.
Skt.
Vester
Vester Farimagsgade
H. C. Andersen
Hammerichsg.
Frederiks-holms Canal
Vindebrog.
Børsgade
5 6 7, Frederiksberg, Zoo
Town Hall
Vesterbrogade
Vesterport Station
Stromg.
Ny Vesterg.
SLOTSHOLMEN
Gammel Kongevej
Banegårds-pladsen
Bernstorffs-gade
Dante Plads
Christians Brygge
VESTERBRO
Vesterbrogade
Main Station
Boulevard
Inderhavnen
Absalons-gade
Istedgade
Tietgengade
ROUTE 1
COPENHAGEN
Kalvebod Brygge
Langebro
Amager Bld.
0
500m
N
1 2 3 4 8 9 10 11 12 13 14 15 16 17 18 19 20 21 22 23 28 29 30 40 41 42 43 44 45

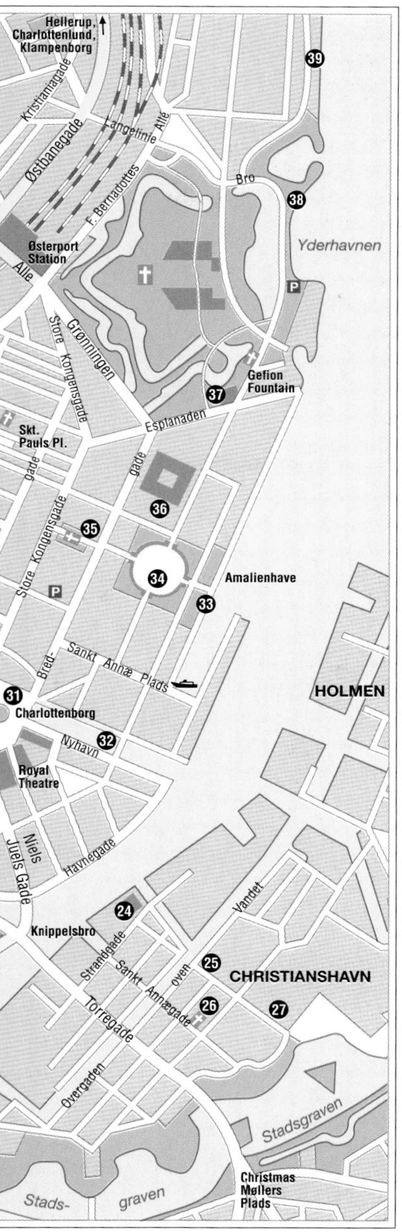

Sights in Copenhagen

1. Town Hall Square
2. Tivoli Gardens
3. Tycho Brahe Planetarium
4. Municipal Museum
5. Fredirksberg Have
6. Carlsberg brewery
7. Royal Copenhagen Porcelain Manufactory
8. Carlsberg Glyptotek
9. National Museum
10. Folketing (Parliament)
11. Royal Chambers
12. Christiansborg Palace Tower
13. Royal Mews
14. Coach Museum
15. Theatre Museum
16. Palace Chapel
17. Thorvaldsen Museum
18. Gammel Strand
19. Christiansborg Slotsplads
20. Holmenskirke
21. Royal Library
22. Arsenal
23. Exchange
24. Gammel Dok
25. Naval Museum
26. Church of Our Saviour
27. Christiana Free State
28. Strøget
29. Museum of Erotica
30. Grabrødretorv
31. King's New Square
32. Nyhavn
33. Harbour Promenade
34. Amalienborg Palace
35. Marmorkirken
36. Museum of Decorative and Applied Arts
37. Freedom Museum
38. Little Mermaid
39. Langliniekaj
40. Church of Our Lady
41. Round Tower
42. Workers' Museum
43. Rosenborg Palace
44. State Art Museum
45. Hirschsprung Samling

'Lur Players' and the town hall tower
Preceding pages: Nyhavn waterfront

Route 1

Copenhagen

Denmark's capital – and the cultural capital of Europe in 1996 – is the country's undisputed metropolis. It is the residence of the queen, the seat of government, parliament and the supreme court, the centre of the media, a major Scandinavian traffic junction, the centre of trade and industry – and it is also strikingly colourful and relaxed.

However, Copenhagen is not that central geographically: it is situated in the northeast of the country on the island of Sjælland, opposite the Swedish industrial centre around Malmö. The historic connections across the Sound *(see page 11)* have remained, and a Scandinavian super-metropolis known as *Ørestad* is already being planned for the 21st century, connected on both sides of the Sound by a system of bridges and tunnels.

Copenhagen itself *(Københavns Kommune)* has a population of only 470,000, but the independent town of Frederiksberg (pop. 86,000) is just a few yards west of the main station, and statisticians also include the northern town of Gentofte (pop. 65,000) in their calculations. And that's not all: the three towns making up the capital combine with 25 other municipalities to form Greater Copenhagen with 1.337 million inhabitants.

Sightseeing starts here

Copenhagen, founded in 1167 by Bishop Absalon, who built a castle on the site (made into a royal residence by King Erik VII in 1417) was surrounded by fortifications until well into the 19th century. It was only from 1852 onwards, after the industrial revolution had demanded greater living space than could be provided by the cramped medieval centre, that the city finally spread beyond the constrictions of its defensive walls. These walls ran from the castleas far as the harbour and can still be clearly made out in Christianshavn.

Town Hall Square is the hub of the city's bus traffic

Walk 1

From the Town Hall Square to Frederiksberg

Copenhagen's ★ **Town Hall Square** *(Rådhuspladsen)* ❶ is the centre of bus traffic in the city, and all the sightseeing tours begin next to the statue of the Viking Lur Blowers. The ★ **Town Hall** (1905), built in Italian Renaissance style, has a golden figure of the city's founder, Bishop Absalon, above its portal. The 105-m (344-ft) high ★ **tower** can be climbed.

On the other side of Hans Christian Andersen Boulevard are the ★★ **Tivoli Gardens** ❷ (main entrance at Vesterbrogade 3), one of the most famous amusement parks in the world and by far the most popular sight in Denmark. The gardens were founded in 1844 by Georg Carstensen, and a museum documenting their history is situated in the Hans Christian Andersen Palace (Hans Christian Andersens Boulevard 22). The gardens contain modern carousels and amusement halls, shooting galleries, restaurants of every price category, cafés and pubs, and also several theatres featuring a range of plays, including traditional pantomime. However, it is the festive way in which the Tivoli Gardens are laid out, with their flowers, fountains and evening illumination by thousands of lights, that gives them their special charm.

This way to the Tivoli Gardens

Adjoining the busy Vesterbrogade is the interesting square known as **Axeltorv**, which contains Robert Jakobsen's 1988 sculpture *De Syv Axler*. Moving further out of town the route passes the **main station** *(Hovedbanegård)*. Several tourist hotels can be found along the next section of the Vesterbrogade. The Isledgade, which runs parallel, is the last refuge of the city's once-infamous pornography trade. Another parallel street further north is dominated by the huge **Tycho Brahe Planetarium** ❸ (Gammel Kongevej 10), named after the Danish astronomer Tycho Brahe (1546–1601), to whom an exhibition is devoted. The planetarium contains state-of-the-art equipment including an Omnimax cinema screen.

Axeltorv Square

The **Municipal Museum** ❹ *(Københavns Bymuseum*, Vesterbrogade 59) documents the history of Copenhagen and also has a small exhibition devoted to to the philosopher Søren Kierkegaard (1813–55). There is a scale model of the city as it looked in medieval times in the courtyard outside the museum entrance. The Absalonsgade nearby is a museum street, with kiosks, lanterns, hydrants, etc dating from 1850–1940.

Lazing on a sunny afternoon

The Carlsberg Brewery

A little further on is **Frederiksberg**, which contains one of the most popular Sunday destinations among locals, the generously laid-out park known as the **Frederiksberg Have** ❺. At the edge of the park is the famous ★★ **Zoo** (Roskildevej 32) and Frederiksberg Palace. You will also find some popular, traditional-style pubs which are a good place to stop for a drink. A maze was planted here in preparation for Copenhagen's turn as the European City of Culture year in 1996.

The ★ **Carlsberg Brewery** ❻ offers conducted tours on weekdays which include the chance to taste its beer. The brewery buildings, especially the gatehouse, are fine examples of turn-of-the-century industrial architecture.

The **Royal Copenhagen Porcelain Manufactory** (Smallegade 45) ❼ also offers conducted tours on weekdays. Visitors are especially attracted by the reasonable prices of its 'seconds'.

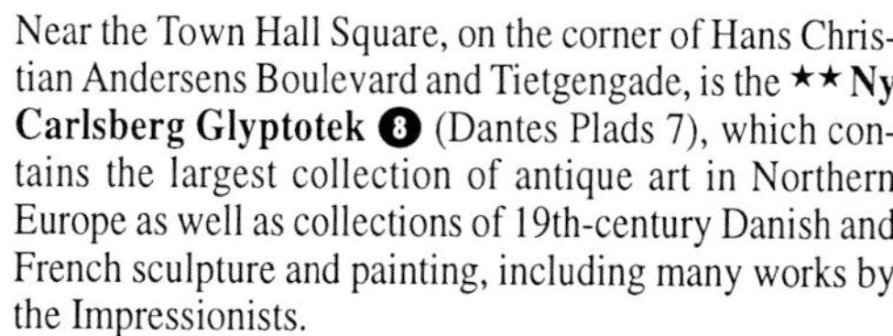

Walk 2

From the Town Hall Square to Christianshavn

Gardens of the National Museum

Near the Town Hall Square, on the corner of Hans Christian Andersens Boulevard and Tietgengade, is the ★★ **Ny Carlsberg Glyptotek** ❽ (Dantes Plads 7), which contains the largest collection of antique art in Northern Europe as well as collections of 19th-century Danish and French sculpture and painting, including many works by the Impressionists.

Cross the Dante Plads now to reach the ★★ **National Museum** *(Nationalmuseet)* ❾ (main entrance at Ny Vestergade 10), the most important cultural-historical museum in the country. The collections document Danish history chronologically. Among the outstanding exhibits

Gunderstrup silver kettle in the National Museum

is the famous ★★ **Trundholm Sun Chariot** *(see page 73)*. The ethnological section also provides a fascinating glimpse into other cultures. The museum includes an exhibition especially for children.

The National Museum is bordered to the north by the Frederiksholms Canal, spanned by the **Marble Bridge** (1775) which leads to the 'castle islet' of ★★ **Slotsholmen,** the centre of power in the state of Denmark and packed with interesting sights. ★ **Christiansborg** has been occupied since 1928 by the ***Folketing* (Parliament)** ❿, the Supreme Court, the Foreign Office and the **Royal Chambers** ⓫ (guided tours).

Christiansborg Palace

The palace is the fifth to be built on the site. The foundations of Absalon's original structure dating from the 12th century can still be viewed in the basement of the **tower** ⓬. In the side wing near the **Royal Mews** ⓭ is a fascinating **coach museum** ⓮, and the former court theatre appropriately contains a **theatre museum** ⓯.

On the side of the castle island facing the city centre is the neoclassical **palace chapel** ⓰, recently restored after a fire in 1992. Next door to it, the ★★ **Thorvaldsen Museum** ⓱ is devoted to the work of Danish neoclassical sculptor Bertel Thorvaldsen (1770–1844), who also lies buried here. A frieze on the outer walls shows the artist's return to Copenhagen from his decades-long 'exile' in Rome. One of the finest views of the city can be enjoyed from here, facing the city centre from the museum and looking across at Gammel Strand ⓲, the quay where the harbour round-trip boats dock.

Whenever demonstrations take place in Copenhagen they are always held on the **Christiansborg Slotsplads** ⓳. The equestrian statue in the square is of Frederick VII, staring across the canal in the direction of the **Holmenskirke** ⓴. This naval church, originally built in 1619, was commissioned by King Christian IV.

The Exchange Building

On the side of the castle island facing the harbour is the **Royal Library** ㉑, built in 1906, as well as several other buildings commissioned by Christian IV: the **Royal Brewery**, with its oversized tiled roof; the **Arsenal** ㉒, which contains an exhibition of weaponry; and one of the finest Renaissance buildings in Copenhagen, the ★ **Exchange** *(Børsen)* ㉓, the spire of which, with its intertwined dragons' tails, is a distinctive feature of the city skyline.

Passing the Exchange, it's worth making a short detour to the island of **Amager**, the location not only of the city's international airport but also of the picturesque harbour town of **Dragør** (ferries to Sweden) and, on the opposite side of the harbour basin, the section of the capital known as **Christianshavn**, a kind of mini-Amsterdam complete with idyllic canals and some fine old houses. This part of the city is also the home of the Exhibition Centre for

Christianshavn

Architecture and Design known as **Gammel Dok** ㉔ (Strandgade 27B), as well as the ★ **Naval Museum** ㉕ (Overgaden oven Vandet 58).

High above it all is the unusual-looking tower of the **Church of Our Saviour** *(Vor Frelsers Kirke)* ㉖ (Sankt Annægade), with its exterior spiral staircase (reopened in 1995 after renovation).

Drumming in Christiana Free State

The **Christiana Free State** ㉗, a 'social experiment' started by some squatters in 1971, runs along parts of the former city fortifications. It has gained official sanction and has now become the model for several similar experiments by young dropouts across Europe. Bordering the area to the north is the former naval base of **Holmen**, a large, attractive open space covering 50ha (123 acres) which was bequeathed to the city of Copenhagen by the Danish navy at the beginning of the 1990s. Its future is not yet clear, but alongside the offices and apartments that are due to be built here are some 20 listed buildings from the mid-19th century.

Walk 3

From the Town Hall Square to the Little Mermaid

The Town Hall Square marks the start of the 1.8-km (1-mile) long pedestrian precinct called the ★ **Strøget** ㉘. Composed of various streets and squares, it runs through the centre of the city; the ★ **Amagertorv** is the square at its centre, and is adorned with a century-old fountain decorated with the shapes of storks. The house at No 6, Amagertorv with the distinctive Renaissance gable, contains the city's main exhibition halls and sales rooms of **Royal Porcelain.** Several other streets to the right and left (Købmagergade, Strædet) have been turned into traffic-free zonesa.

The **Museum of Erotica** ㉙ (Købmagergade 24) owes its existence to the role Denmark played in the liberalisation of pornography at the end of the 1970s. More suitable for families, perhaps, is the **Toy Museum** (Legetøjsmuseum) just round the corner at Valkendorfsgade 13). One particularly pleasant square, almost always full of life and lined with 18th-century burghers' houses and popular pubs, is the ★ **Grabrødretorv** ㉚.

The Royal Theatre

The Strøget itself finally reaches ★ **King's New Square** *(Kongens Nytorv)* ㉛, laid out in the 17th century; among the buildings here are the **Royal Theatre** (1874) and the Dutch-baroque mansion of ★ **Charlottenborg** (1672–83). The latter has housed the Royal Academy of Fine Arts since 1753. At the centre of the square is **Krinsen**, an island of green with a baroque equestrian statue of Charles V at its centre.

Nyhavn waterfront

Opposite the Strøget, the Kongens Nytorv is bordered by the picturesque branch canal called ★★ **Nyhavn** ㉜. Today this harbour extension, carried out in 1673, is a popular mooring place for several antique sailing vessels, and there are so many fine pubs along this canal that it's difficult to make up one's mind which one to visit. Hans Christian Andersen loved this busy, colourful part of the city, and lived for a while at three different addresses here (Nyhavn 18, 20 and 67).

The route now turns to the right at the end of the canal and heads north past the ferry docks to the★★ **Harbour Promenade** ㉝, which has been under restoration for several years now. At the beginning of the route is a former granary (1780), today the Copenhagen Admiral Hotel.

In front of the West Indies Warehouse, dating from 1781, is the 6-m (20-ft) high bronze copy of ★ **Michelangelo's *David***. The warehouse contains the **Den Kongelige Afstøbingssamling**, a collection of 2,000 plaster casts of famous sculptures from ancient Egypt.

Amalienborg Palace

The park of Amalienhave, already mentioned above, separates the harbour from ★★ **Amalienborg Palace** ㉞, the residence of the Danish royal family. The palace was built between 1749 and 1760 by Nicolai Eigtved, whose design was French-inspired. The four identical rococo palaces were originally planned for noble families, but were taken over by the royal family when Christiansborg burnt down in 1794.

Changing of the Guard

The **Christian VIII Palace** has been open to the public since April 1994 as the Glücksburger Museum and is a continuation of the Rosenborg Collections (*see page 25*) from the epoch of Christian IX (1863–1906). If the queen is present, the Changing of the Guard takes place on the palace square at 12 noon with a great deal of ceremony. The equestrian statue (1771) at the centre of the square

The dome of the Marmorkirken

is of Frederick V; he appears to be riding towards the dome of the ★ **Marmorkirken** ❸❺, otherwise known as Frederiks Kirke. The construction of the church lasted a full 150 years – it was only in 1894 that a patron finally provided enough money for its completion, and even then it was one-third smaller than planned and comprised a lot more limestone than marble.

The route continues via the Bredgade to the ★★ **Museum of Decorative and Applied Arts** *(Kunstindustriemuseet)* ❸❻, founded in 1890, with exhibitions of craft and design from the Late Middle Ages to the present and also the best collection of Japanese arts and crafts anywhere in the world outside Japan. The huge 4.6-m (15-ft) high vase by Peter Brandes in the courtyard is also the symbol of the museum.

The Little Mermaid

Follow the esplanade from the end of the Bredgade in the direction of the harbour, and soon the **Freedom Museum** *(Frihedsmuseet)* ❸❼ comes into view. It documents the efforts of the Danish Resistance against the Germans during World War II. The route then continues past the English church and the imposing-looking Gefion Fountain and arrives at the Langelinie Promenade with its famous ★★ **Little Mermaid** *(Lille Havfrue)* ❸❽, the life-sized sculpture created by Edvard Eiksen in 1913, based on a motif from Hans Christian Andersen's fairy-tale. The figure is modelled on the sculptor's wife.

Further inland, hidden behind green ramparts and moats, is the **Citadel** *(Kastellet)*, a fortification dating from the time of Christian IV. Further along the embankment from the Mermaid is the **Langliniekaj** ❸❾; cruise ships dock here, and the quay is due to be redesigned by Jørn Utzon *(see page 80)*. Protecting the harbour entrance opposite is **Fort Trekkonrer** (1787), one of three islands formerly fortified to protect Copenhagen from naval attack, and today an increasingly popular location for cultural events and excursions. The two other islands, lying further out in the Sound, are **Flakfortet** (1916) and the largest artificial island in the world, **Middelgrunds Fort** (1894).

Church of Our Lady

Walk 4

From the Town Hall Square to the State Art Museum

From the Town Hall Square it's only a few metres along the Strøget to the **Old Square** *(Gammel Torv)*, with its playful Caritas Fountain (1608). From here the neo-classical **Church of Our Lady** *(Vor Frue Kirke)* ❹⓿, completed in 1829, becomes visible. It contains sculptures by Thorvaldsen, Bissen and Jerichau. Directly next to the church is the old **University Library** and on the other

side, behind a high wall, the **Sankt Petri Kirke** – the oldest church in Copenhagen.

The Krystalgade now leads to the ★ **Round Tower** *(Runde Tårn)* ❹❶ on Købmagergade. It was built during the reign of Christian IV. The main attraction of the tower is not the tiny observatory at the top but the ascent itself, along a 209-m (685-ft) long ramp without any steps, except for the ones at the very end just before the observation platform.

Taking in the sights from the Round Tower

Ascent is via the ramp

Leave the tower now and cross the modern square known as Kultorvet to the underground station of **Nørreport**. Close to here and definitely worth a visit is the **Workers' Museum** *(Arbejdermuseet)* ❹❷, documenting the history of the working classes from the late 19th century. In an 1892-style beer hall, traditional food and drink can be purchased at modern prices.

Around 1.5km (1 mile) away from here, via Frederiksborggade and Nørrebrogade, is the section of Copenhagen known as Nørrebro, which contains the finest cemetery in the city: the **Assistenz Kirkegård**. Several famous Danes are buried here, including Hans Christian Andersen and Martin Andersen Nexø.

North of Nørreport Station, to the left of the Øster Voldgade, is the **Botanical Garden**, which boasts an especially fine palm house, and to the right is ★★ **Rosenborg Palace** *(Rosenborg Slot)* ❹❸. Built in Dutch Renaissance style between 1606 and 1617, the palace contains a series of apartments, laid out chronologically, documenting the various regencies from Christian IV (1588) to Frederick IV (1863). The Danish crown jewels are on display here too. Rosenborg is on the edge of the Kongens Have park, which is very popular for recreation and relaxation in the summertime.

Rosenborg Palace Gardens

Beyond the junction of Øster Voldgade and Solvgade it's hard to miss the complex of buildings making up the

State Art Museum

newly renovated ★★ **State Art Museum** *(Statens Museum for Kunst)* ㊹, representing all the important Scandinavian and European art movements from the 14th century onwards. Beyond it, in the Østre Anlæg Park, the **Hirschsprung Samling** ㊺ (Stockholmsgade 20) features predominantly 19th-century Danish art.

Sights in the Suburbs

On the way out of the city centre to the coast road heading north, in the section of the city known as **Hellerup** (6km/3.7 miles), is the **Tuborg Brewery** (conducted tours on weekdays), which even has its own harbour. A special attraction is its bottling hall which contains the *Eksperimentarium*, where visitors of all ages can carry out natural science experiments.

In Copenhagen's fashionable suburb of **Charlottenlund** (10km/6 miles), a day at the races or at the fine bathing resort can be combined with a visit to the aquarium *(Danmarks Akvarium)*.

Further north the Strandvej becomes a real coast road, and soon arrives at the suburb of **Klampenborg** (14km/8 miles, also accessible by rail). The seawater swimming pool of **Bellevue** is one of the most popular pools in the Sound. Close to here, those interested in architecture will find a large residential complex and theatre designed in the 1930s by Arne Jakobsen *(see page 80)*.

Bakken fun park and the Giant Teapot Ride

During summer months, the large wildlife sanctuary of ★★ **Dyrehaven**, the Eremitagen hunting-lodge and ★★ **Bakken**, which is the oldest amusement park in Denmark (March to August), are ideal destinations for day trips from Copenhagen. **Peter Lieps'** rustic restaurant in the forest is the place where the locals go to drink hot chocolate after winter walks.

Kongens Lyngby (15km/9 miles, also accessible by rail) is a suburb with a population of around 50,000. The old part of the town nestling around the church forms an unexpected and pleasant contrast to the modern architecture elsewhere. Particular attractions of the area include ★ **boat trips** on antique sailing vessels across the lakes of Lyngby SØ, Bagsværd SØ and Furre SØ, where canoes can also be hired.

The country manor of ★ **Sophienholm**, on the banks of Bagsværd SØ, can be reached by boat and also by car; today it is used for exhibitions. Among the few works permanently on display are the ceiling fresco *Cobra Loftet*, a joint work by CoBrA artists *(see page 80)*, and also a mammoth vase by Peter Brandes.

To the north of Kongens Lyngby lie a number of attractions that shouldn't be missed: the old textile factory

of ★ **Brede** (in operation from 1783 right up until 1956) is considered the cradle of Danish industrialisation. Today it forms part of the National Museum, its collection concentrating on industrialisation and textiles. The museum also hosts large temporary exhibitions on a variety of themes.

Next door to this the ★★ **Sorgenfri Open-Air Museum** contains reconstructions of typical Danish houses from different parts of the country. And the ★ **Mølleådalen** (Millstream Valley), the first industrial region in Denmark to have been placed under environmental protection, is an oasis of tranquillity.

The route now continues from Lyngby via Birkerød to **Hillerød** (37km/22 miles, pop. 25,000; also accessible by rail), situated at the heart of northern Sjælland. On the outskirts of the town is ★★ **Frederiksberg Palace**, which like many other fine Renaissance structures in Denmark dates back to the reign of Christian IV. It was rebuilt after a fire in 1859 thanks to the financial support of the Jacobsen brewing dynasty. Today it houses the Museum of Danish National History.

The palace chapel, which escaped the fire, is particularly beautiful. It contains an original Compenius organ (built in 1610) and it makes a fine setting for concerts held in July and August. Apart from the chapel, the most notable rooms are the Council Hall and the Knights' Hall, where the walls are hung with shields presented by many famous visitors.

North of the castle's lake is one of the best-preserved baroque gardens in Northern Europe, and to the west is a large English garden with a small Renaissance chapel (1581) which Frederick II used as a bath house. In summer it is pleasant to take a boat trip on the castle lake.

Interior exhibit at Sorgenfri Open-Air Museum

Sorgenfri: seaweed thatches

Frederiksberg Palace was renovated after the 1859 fire

Route 2

Opposite: view from Ribe Cathedral

Along Jutland's North Sea Coast: Tønder – Ribe – Holmsland Klit – Thyborøn – Hanstholm – Hjørring – Hirtshals – Skagen (475km/295 miles)

From the German border to Skagen, this route combines the attractions of pretty harbour towns with the wild beauty of a coastline that includes drifting dunes and impressive cliffs.

★ **Tønder** (pop. 8,000, *see also* Route 6, *page 47*), 5km (3 miles), was an important harbour town until the 16th century, and a centre of European lace-making in the 17th century. The burghers' houses with their magnificent portals testify to the wealth of the lace merchants of that time. The town centre is dominated by the 50-m (164-ft) high tower of the **Kristkirke**, originally a navigational landmark and older than the richly-ornamented 16th-century church itself. On the outskirts of the town is a museum complex containing the **Tønder Museum** (exhibits include examples of lace-making) and the ★ **Sønderjyllands Kunstmuseum** (20th-century art, especially Danish surrealists). The Tønder Festival of folk music takes place at the end of August each year.

In **Brøns**, the Romanesque ★ **village church** contains a cycle of frescoes that has been interpreted as a bold defence of Protestantism during the time of the Reformation.

Soon the side-road branches off in the direction of Vester Vedsted, from where, at low tide, the Mandø bus travels across to the island of ★ **Mandø** with its mud-flats. This makes an ideal day trip.

★★ **Ribe** (pop. 7,500), 52km (32 miles) is the oldest town in Denmark (first mentioned in records in 860), and with its brick and half-timbered houses dating from the 16th and 17th centuries has retained its historic character. The hallmark of the city is its five-aisled ★★ **Cathedral**, part of which is 12th-century Romanesque. The choir was decorated in a very modern manner (glass mosaics, frescoes and windows) by CoBrA artist Carl-Henning Petersen *(see page 80)*. There is an excellent view of the town from the top of the ★ **tower**, built in 1333.

To the west of Varde (pop. 12,000, with amusement park and ★ medieval model village), 91km (56 miles), are several fine beaches and holiday home areas along the coast, eg Henne Strand. A gastronomic tip: in the summer, Denmark's famous TV chef Hans Beck Thomsen runs the **Henne Kirkeby Kro**

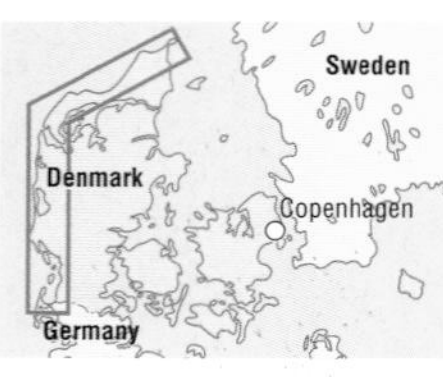

directly next to the church in the village of the same name. It's one of the best restaurants on the west coast of Jutland (tel: 75-255-400).

The route reaches the coast again at **Nymindegab**, 122km (75 miles). The Ringkøbing Fjord was connected to the North Sea here until the last century by a tidal current. Along the edge of the road traditional 19th-century fishing huts have been restored to their original state. North of the settlement, on the flat Tipperne peninsula, is a bird sanctuary (observation tower).

A paradise for windsurfers

Travel on from here for another 35km (21 miles) across the narrow sand bar known as ★★ **Holmsland Klit**, which separates the North Sea from the surfing paradise of Ringkøbing Fjord. Holmsland Klit is one of the country's most popular holiday and camping regions. An artificial connection between Ringkøbing Fjord and the North Sea was created in 1931 near **Hvide Sande** (pop. 3,400), 143km (88 miles). This attractive fishing village grew up close to the mighty system of sluices here (★ fish auctions held on weekdays at 7am). There is a fine view of the coastal panorama from the 38-m (125-ft) high lighthouse of ★ **Nørre Lyngvig**, slightly to the north.

Nørre Lyngvig Lighthouse

Søndervig, 156km (96 miles, *see also* Route 8, *page* 52), is a typical west-coast bathing resort, with hardly any local inhabitants but a great number of holiday homes and apartment complexes.

Road 181 carries on beyond the dunes, which rise as high as 30m (110ft) in places, affording magnificent views across the Stadils Fjord. This fjord is a well-known stopover for migrating birds, and large sections of the surrounding landscape have been reclaimed. A typical farm in this region is the ★ **Strandgården**, 165km (102 miles), built in 1875 and now a museum.

The view from Bovbjerg Fyr

Torsminde, 188km (116 miles), is a small fishing village between the Nissum Fjord and the North Sea, and its ★★ **Strandungsmuseum St George** contains finds from shipwrecks, in particular from the vessel involved in the worst catastrophe ever to have occurred off Denmark's west coast: on Christmas Eve in 1811, a hurricane drove two British naval vessels on to the rocks near Torsminde, and 1,300 sailors were drowned. Near **Ferring**, 207km (128 miles), there is a fine section of steep and rocky coastline, especially impressive where it reaches 41m (135ft) at the ★ **Bovbjerg**; it is best viewed from the lighthouse of ★ **Bovbjerg Fyr**.

Shipwreck survivor

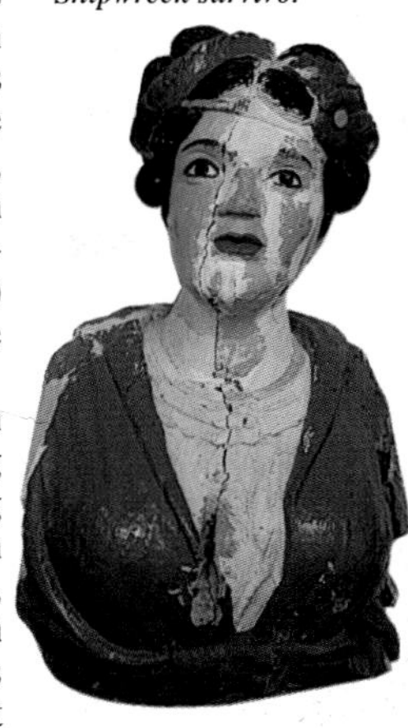

On the promontory of Harboør Tange lies **Thyborøn** (pop. 2,800), 235km (146 miles), an important fishing harbour at the mouth of the Limfjord. In the town and along the beach, numerous German bunkers still remain from World War II. They formed part of the 'Atlantic Wall', built between 1943 and 1944. A **Bunker Museum** documents their significance, and a ★ **Bunker Path** leads between the various fortifications. A refreshing contrast to the grim military architecture here is the imaginative 'snail house', the result of years of work by a Thyborøn native who decorated it with shells.

The snail house

The car ferry (departures twice hourly; journey time 10 minutes) crosses the Thyborøn Canal, which connects the Limfjord and the North Sea. The ★★ **Limfjord** runs across Jutland from the North Sea to the Baltic, and has become a mecca for water-sports enthusiasts because of its excellent surfing and sailing facilities. It is also a paradise for nature lovers: the smaller islands in particular, as well as the ★ **Vejlerne**, a former arm of the fjord between Thisted and Fjerritslev in the north, are bird sanctuaries of international importance.

An alternative to the ferry crossing is the land route via the Oddesund Bridge further to the east. It leads first to picturesque **Lemvig**, situated on a bay. The **planet route** (12km/7 miles) which runs from Lemvig to the bank of the Nissum Bredning, features large-scale models of the planets of the solar system.

North of the industrial town of Struer – home of the internationally famous hi-fi firm of Bang & Olufsen, founded in 1925 – turn northwards and head via the Oddesund Bridge and Thyholm to the region of Thy. This area, particularly its southern section, is strewn with prehistoric monuments and sites. For example, on the moor of ★ **Ydby Hede** there are 50 Bronze Age burial mounds.

Whichever route you choose, both meet up at **Vestervig**, 247km (153 miles). This village was one of Denmark's most important medieval settlements, a bishop's see with its own monastery and cathedral. When the mouth of the Limfjord silted up at the end of the 11th century,

Liden Kirstens' grave

Nørre Vorupør resort

Vestervig lost its earlier importance and today the only reminders of its former glory are the largest village church in Northern Europe and the legendary grave of Liden Kirstens, sister of Valdemar the Great.

Road 181 continues along the dune-lined coast. There are only a few bathing resorts here; one is Nørre Vorupør, 267km (165 miles), another is Klitmøller (which is one of the best ★ surfing resorts in Europe), 281km (174 miles). After passing the Hanstholm Wildlife Reservation (a treeless heathland rich in bird and wildlife: limited access) the route arrives at **Hanstholm** (pop. 2,700), 291km (180 miles), which developed after the construction of its harbour in 1967. The old lighthouse, visible for miles around, has one of the most powerful lamps in the world (4000w). There are also cannon emplacements dating from World War II (in the museum).

The main route now leads from Hanstholm to Fjerritslev (pop. 3,200; brewery museum). Between Øsløs and Fjerritslev it's worth making a short detour to the 47-m (155-ft) high ★ **Bulbjerg**, a limestone cliff offering a magnificent view across the North Sea and the surrounding beaches. The ★ **Vejlerne bird sanctuary** *(see page 31)* is also on this route. Another interesting detour: at the southern outskirts of Fjerritslev, turn south and cross the Limfjord at Aggersund. On the north bank, fragments of the **Aggersborg** have been preserved; it was once the largest Viking fort in the north and had a diameter of 240m (790ft; compared to a mere 120m/390ft in the case of the Fyrkat fort, *see page 39*).

ROUTES 2 and 4 (northern part)

The main route leads from Fjerritslev via Brovst to Åbybro, 367km (228 miles), and shortly after that it turns north again to the coast. Popular bathing resorts here include **Blokhus** (good amusement park for children near Saltum) and **Lokken**, 388km (241 miles). The area is very popular with campers: there are 19 campsites spread across 25km (15 miles) of beach.

High on a hill somewhat inland from Lokken is ★ **Børglum Monastery** with its mighty church; it was the bishop's see of northern Jutland from around 1135, but fell into secular hands at the time of the Reformation (some sections are open to the public).

Instead of travelling on to Hjørring directly, it's possible to turn off to Lønstrup just inside Sønder Rudbjerg, 395km (247 miles). The ★★ **Rudbjerg Knude** sand-dunes (74km/45 miles), which have already partially blocked the view from the Rudbjerg Fyr lighthouse (★ sand museum), and the Romanesque Mårup Kirke high up on the cliffs are two good reasons for making the detour; another is the little bathing resort of ★ **Lønstrup** itself.

Hjørring (pop. 24,000) contains a local museum (★ Vendsyssels Historiks Museum), an art museum and three Romanesque churches. The square known as ★ **P Norskjærs Plads** with its modern sculpture by Bjørn Nørgaard is also worth looking round.

Sculpture in Hjørring

Hirtshals (pop. 7,000), 425km (264 miles), still relies on its harbour and fishery, a small shipyard and a ferry to Norway for its livelihood. The big attraction here is the ★★ **Nordsømuseum** with its salt-water aquarium and seal pool.

Along the coast of Tannis Bay near Tversted is a popular 'car beach', where cars can be driven right up to the water's edge. The ★★ **eagle observation area** at Tuen, 448km (278 miles), does falconry demonstrations up to twice a week during the season.

The route reaches the Baltic coast near Ålbæk and then turns northwards on to the Skagen peninsula. Near Hulsig, 462km (287 miles), is the vehicle entrance to the drifting sand dune of ★★ **Råbjerg Mile**, 800m (2,625ft) wide and 2km (1 mile) long, moving eastwards by as much as 20m (65ft) every year.

The St Lawrence tower

★★ **Skagen** (pop. 12,000), 475km (295 miles), is Denmark's northernmost town. Its harbour (★ fish auctions once or twice a day during the week) and museums lie on the Baltic side, and the rather cosmopolitan bathing resort of Gammel Skagen lies on the North Sea side. In 1795 Skagen was forced to abandon its church of St Lawrence (★ Den tilsandede Kirke) because it was threatened by sand drift. Today its tower is the symbol of the town. The Skagen Group of painters *(see page 80)* congregated here at the turn of the century and made the town famous; the ★★ **Skagen Museum** contains examples of their work.

The Skagens Fortidsminder open-air museum has information about local history, in particular about the fishing community here in earlier times, while the **Museum of Natural History** housed in the old Højen railway station on the south side of town documents the unique natural landscape of the area.

Natural History Museum sign

Continental Europe's northernmost point, ★★ **Grenen**, lies just 5 minutes from Skagen. Special buses transport tired hikers the last few kilometres from the car park out to the sandy point where the custom is to stand with one foot in the North Sea and the other in the Baltic (NB: swimming here is prohibited because of dangerous currents).

The Grenen art museum contains various examples of maritime art, and among the dunes nearby is the grave of the writer and painter Holger Drachmann *(Drachmanns Grav)*, considered to be the founding father of the Skagen artists' colony.

Route 3

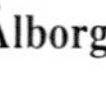

Ålborg

With a population of 115,000, Ålborg, or Aalborg as the locals prefer to spell it, is Denmark's fourth-largest town. There was an important settlement here on the Limfjord as long ago as the Bronze and Viking ages, and the Lindholm Høje necropolis stands as a memorial to it. Ålborg's favourable geographic location made it a powerful trading centre from very early on – it was granted its charter in 1342 – and later helped it become an important industrial city. Aalborger Akvavit, the Dane's fiery national drink (a caraway-flavoured schnapps), is the town's most famous export article.

CW Obels Plads, Ålborg

Sights

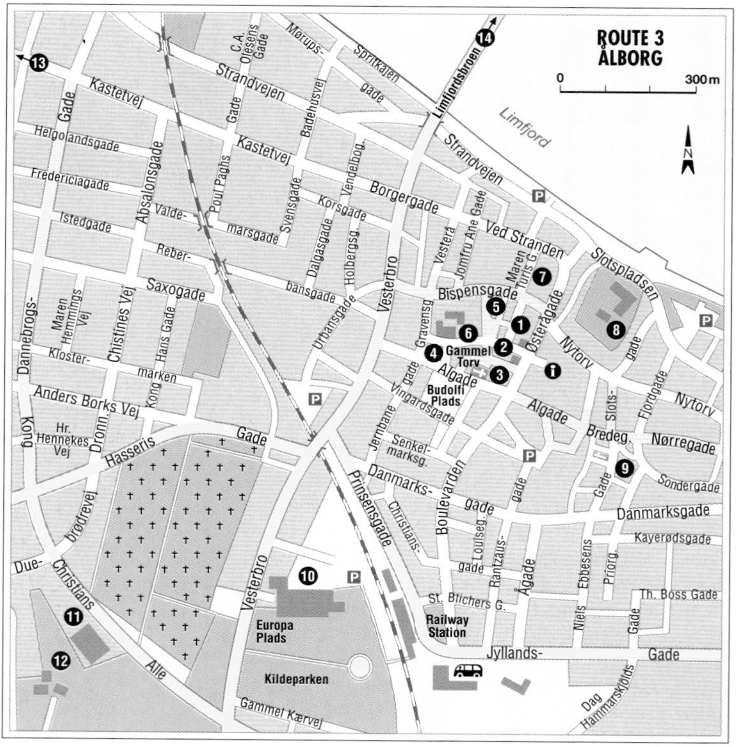

Opposite the information office, the ★★ **Jens Bangs Stenhus** ❶ (Ostergade 9), built in 1624, is considered the finest burgher's house in Northern Europe and testifies to the degree of wealth enjoyed by the merchants of Ålborg at that time. Legend has it that Bang, the merchant

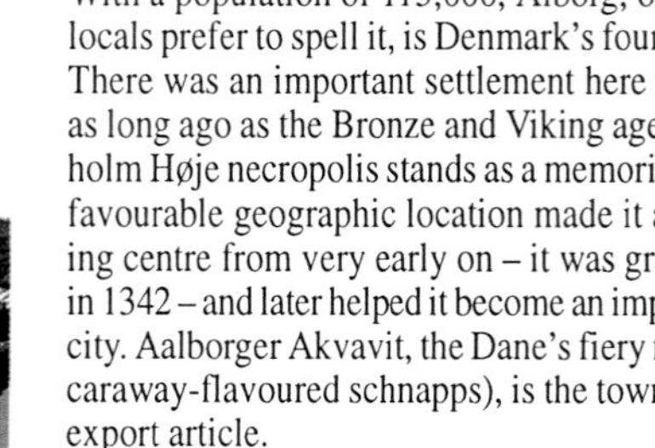

who built the house, gave full vent to his frustration at not having been voted on to the city council by adding a cheeky face to the southern gable of the house with its tongue sticking out in the direction of the neighbouring **Town Hall** ❷ *(Gammel Torv)*, built in late baroque style on the site of an earlier structure in 1762.

The Town Hall

A few steps from here is the baroque-tipped tower of **Budolfi Cathedral** ❸. Built on the remnants of a Romanesque church in 1400, it has undergone several alterations. The fact that the cathedral is consecrated to the English patron saint of sailors, St Botolph, testifies to the importance of the Limfjord region in foreign trade.

Next door to the cathedral is the **Ålborg Historical Museum** *(Aalborgs Historiske Museum)* ❹ (Algade 48), containing a ★ **Renaissance chamber** dating from 1602 and a fine collection of glass. A few steps north of the museum is the large square known as **CW Obels Plads** ❺, in summer filled with tables and chairs from the surrounding cafés and restaurants. Next to it is the **Monastery of the Holy Ghost**, founded in 1431 and today an old people's home – the oldest in Denmark. The historic rooms and frescoes here can be admired in the course of a guided tour (June to August).

Renaissance chamber, Historical Museum

Leave CW Obels Plads now to the north via a passageway leading to the shopping street of Bispensgade. Branching off here is the ★ **Jomfrue Ane Gade** ❻, otherwise known as 'the longest beer counter in Denmark'. Not only pubs are found here: there are also discos, restaurants of varying quality and cafés, some traditional, some ultra-fashionable. At the northern end of the street is the so-called 'friendly casino' (Ved Stranden 14, in the Limfjordshotel) where people can play the tables without having to wear jackets and ties.

The street running parallel to the Jomfrue Ane Gade is the Maren Turisgade. At house No 6 it's possible to cross over to Østerågade 25 via the complex known as ★ **Jørgen Olufsens Gård** ❼. This Renaissance structure, with its half-timbered houses facing the inner courtyard and richly-ornamented stone gable facing Østerågade, is one of the finest buildings in the whole town.

Jørgen Olufsens Gård

Further eastwards along the Limfjord is **Aalborghus Castle** ❽ (Slotspladsen), a half-timbered structure dating from the 16th century. The long drawn-out Nytorv with its modern shops and department stores leads to a parallel street forming the Algade-Bredegade-Nørregade pedestrian precinct, with the **Church of Our Lady** *(Vor Frue Kirke)* ❾. This area contains some of Ålborg's most photogenic streets. The Vesterbrogade passes one of the best-known congress centres in Europe, the **Aalborghallen** ❿ (Europa Plads), with room for up to 8,000 guests. Turn right at the next junction and head for the

Nørgaard's Dream Castle

★★ **North Jutland Museum of Art** *(Nordjyllands Kunstmuseum)* ⓫ (Kong Christians Allé 50). The building itself, completed in 1972, is splendid; the Finnish master architect Alvar Alto had a hand in its design. Its extensive collection of 20th-century art, much of it Danish, is certainly worth a visit. Artworks outside the building, dominated by Bjørn Nørgaard's monumental *Dream Castle*, inspire the imagination.

Up on a hill behind the Museum of Art is the observation tower known as **Aalborgtårnet** ⓬ (Sdr. Skovvej), and a little further south is the town's large ★ **Zoo**.

Naval Museum exhibit

The ★★ **Naval Museum** *(Søfart- og Marinemuseum)* ⓭ (Vestre Fjordvej 81), situated to the west of the city centre on the banks of the Limfjord, is a fascinating place for those keen on seafaring and naval technology. As well as the collection of models, original ships, including a 54-m (177-ft) long submarine, are on display here and can also be boarded.

A very important prehistoric site lies on the other side of the Limfjord near the neighbouring town of Nørresundby: ★★ **Lindholm Høje** ⓮ (Vindilavej 11). It is Northern Europe's largest Iron Age and Viking Age necropolis. A total of 682 graves have been discovered here, 150 of them 'ship monuments' (ie graves enclosed by standing stones in the form of a ship), along with the foundations of some houses. The necropolis was buried by sand drift in around 1050, and re-excavated 900 years later. A museum contains information on the Iron and Viking Ages.

Lindholm Høje necropolis

For more excursions in this area see Route 4, *page 37*.

Route 4

Eastern Jutland: Skagen – Frederikshavn – Ålborg – Randers – Arhus – Horsens – Vejle – Kolding – Haderslev – Abenrå – Kruså (390km/242 miles)

This route leads from Skagen to the German border, along a Baltic Sea coastline characterised by long fjords and broad bays with plenty of safe, sandy beaches. For the northern part of the route, *see map page 32.*

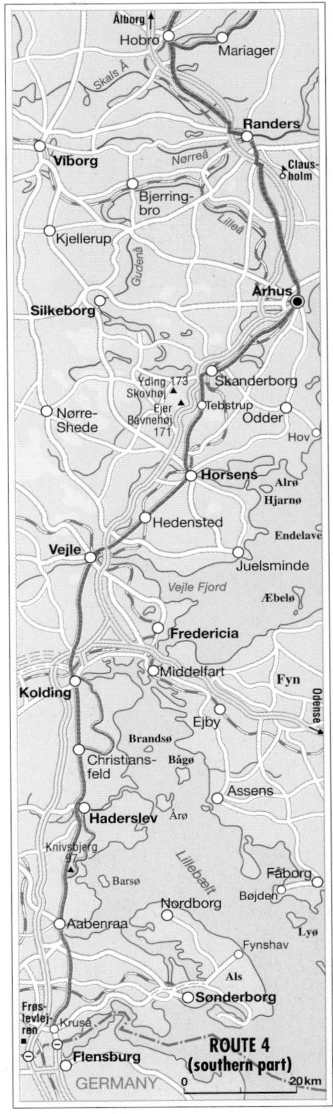

From ★★ **Skagen** (Route 2, *page 33*) the route leads past Ålbæk Bay (holiday homes, beaches, campsites) to the harbour town of **Frederikshavn** (pop. 25,000), 38km (23 miles). Visitors from Sweden and Norway have been an important source of income here in the past, but fluctuating exchange rates have diminished tourism considerably. The local shipyard is also in economic difficulties.

The town's entire powder magazine *(Krudttåmel)* was moved a full 270m (885ft) in 1974. The Fiskerlyngen quarter of town, in which it is situated, dates from the time when Frederikshavn was still known as Fladstrand (until 1818). Closely connected with the Fladstrand Fortress is the name of the maritime hero Peter Wessel (1690–1720), better known as Tordenskjold. Between 1712 and 1717 he defeated several Swedish contingents during the great Nordic War. To the north of the town centre, the Bunker Museum documents the German occupation. The ★ **Bangsbomuseum**, on an 18th-century estate, has collections on cultural themes and also contains the ★ **Ellinga Ship**, a well-preserved Viking ship dating from the 12th century.

Off the coast is the flat Kattegat island of ★★ **Læsø** (pop. 2,500, surface area 10,122ha/25,011 acres), most of which is a conservation area today. The island's original forests were chopped down to provide fuel for the salt-works – an important source of income in Læsø for centuries. Typical of the island are houses with ★ **seaweed roofs** (eg the Byrum Folk Museum). Læsø is a paradise for birds, especially the sandbanks and water meadows in the south.

Sæby (pop. 8,200), 51km (31 miles), has retained much of the charm and atmosphere of its old town. ★ **St Mary's Church**, decorated with Gothic frescoes, is the only surviving part of what used to be a Carmelite monastery (1470). The Renaissance manor house of Sæbygård lies 2km (1 mile) west of it.

★ **Voergård** (near Frauenskjold, 66km/41 miles) is one of the finest Renaissance palaces in Jutland, and contains a magnificent art collection (guided tours).

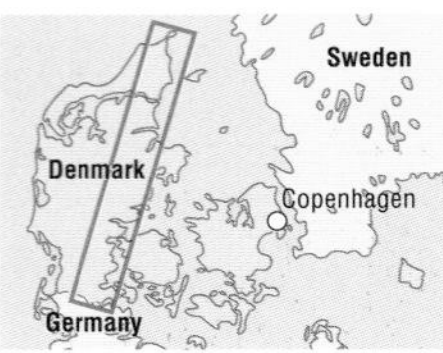

Rold Skov forest

An alternative route leads past the baroque palace of **Dronninglund**. Once a 12th-century Benedictine monastery, it today contains a fine hotel with a good restaurant attached. The route reaches the Baltic coast at **Aså** and then turns southwest through a tourist area with plenty of holiday homes and flat beaches, ideal for children.

A ferry crosses the eastern mouth of the Limfjord at **Hals** (Hals-Egense, several departures every hour, journey time 5 minutes), and then the 541 crosses the bed of what was, in the Stone Age, an ocean. The ★ **Mulbjerge**, which used to be islands, provide a fine view of the flat coastal landscape. The Little Moor *(Lille Vildmose)* somewhat further inland was originally a moor landscape rich in wildlife. **Øster Hurup** contains a modern holiday park with a tropical pool as well as a fine beach. Near Als the route bears round to the west and soon arrives at the town of Hobro on the Mariager Fjord.

The main route now leads from Sæby via Hjallerup, 80km (49 miles), as far as **Ålborg** (103km/64 miles, *see page 34*), the main town of northern Jutland.

★ **Rold Skov**, Denmark's largest forest, extends to the south of Rebild, 128km (79 miles). A museum here devoted to Danish emigration stands as a reminder of all the Danes who left for America and who later founded the **Rebild Bakker National Park** in Rold Skov (every 4 July, the park celebrates American Independence Day, the only celebration outside the United States). The ★ **Troldskov** tree with its fantastically gnarled branches is the subject of many legends.

The main route carries on from here via **Rold** (circus museum) due southwards, but at this point it's worth taking another brief detour along the Daisy Route. It leads via Hadsund and the picturesque village of ★ **Mariager** (ruins of a 15th-century convent) to **Hobro** (pop. 10,000),

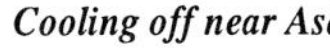

Cooling off near Aså

150km (93 miles). On the southwestern outskirts of this town is one of the most impressive historical sights in Denmark: the Viking fort of ★★ **Fyrkat** with its reconstructed Viking village. The fort, built in around AD980, is surrounded by a wall 120m (393ft) in diameter, enclosing 16 identical longhouses.

Part of Fyrkat Fort

Randers (pop. 55,000), 176km (109 miles, *see also* Route 8, *page 52*), was a market town as long ago as the Middle Ages because of its favoured location at a ford of the Gudenå, Denmark's longest river. There are several fine houses to be seen here, especially the baroque town hall. The stocky-looking Randers House of Culture with its ★ **Museum of Art** (19th- and 20th-century) and **Museum of Cultural History** shows how enthusiastic many provincial Danish towns are where culture is concerned, while the unique underground pipeline system leading straight to taps in the pubs along the Storegade from the local Thor Brewery proves just how thirsty the locals can get – *Skål!*

Museum of Art, Randers

Along the direct route to **Århus** (213km/132 miles, *see page 42*) it's only a short detour to reach the baroque palace of Clausholm, which during the 18th century was the scene of a major society scandal involving royal love affairs, kidnappings, marriages and exile, the main protagonists being Frederick IV and the very young Anna Sophia Reventlow.

From Århus, Route 4 follows the 170. **Skanderborg** (pop. 11,500), 235km (146 miles), lies on the southeast corner of a lake of the same name. It is the area's oldest community, but all that remains of its medieval royal castle is a round tower and the castle church, the latter dating from 1572.

From **Tebstrup**, 244km (151 miles), it's possible to 'scale' Denmark's two highest peaks: the 171m (560ft) high Ejer Bavnehøj, where there is also an observation tower, and the 173m (560ft) high Yding Skovhøj.

★ **Horsens** (pop. 48,000), 258km (160 miles), is one of the most interesting provincial towns in Denmark. A stroll through its spacious pedestrian precinct, the ★ **Søndergade**, the country's broadest thoroughfare, is an experience in itself. Interspersed among the many shops are a number of interesting houses from the 17th and 18th centuries, including the baroque Lichtenberg Place (1744), known today as Jørgensen's Hotel.

The **Church of Our Saviour** *(Vor Frelsers Kirke)* – a 13th-century Gothic brick structure with an ornate interior also dating from the 17th and 18th century – is also situated on the Søndergade. The nearby monastery church is all that remains of a Franciscan monastery built in 1261; its interior is even more ornate than that of the Church of Our Saviour.

Horsens Museum of Art

Den Smidtske Gård

The Koldinghus dates from the 15th century

The ★ **Horsens Museum of Art**, extended in 1992, contains a superb modern section. The ★ **Museum of Craft and Industry**, another excellent museum, documents industrialisation and working conditions at the turn of the century. Next to the Tabaksgården (a former tobacco factory, now a culture complex with a library and gallery) is the monumental equestrian statue *Horseman of the Apocalypse* by Bjørn Nørgaard (*see page 80*), created in 1992.

Horsens' most famous son was Vitus Bering (1681–1741), who explored the straits between Russia and Alaska that now bear his name, while working for the Russians in 1741. There is a memorial plaque in the Vitus Bering park near the railway station.

Vejle (pop. 45,500, 284km/176 miles, *see also* Route 7, *page 50*), an industrial town in an attractive natural environment, lies at the end of the Vejle Fjord which is spanned by a huge 1,710-m (5,600-ft) long motorway bridge built in 1980. The highlight at the centre of the pedestrian precinct here is ★ **Den Smidtske Gård**, a merchant's house dating from 1799 that has recently been renovated. The collection at the Vejle Museum of Art concentrates on graphics. The Late Gothic Church of St Nicholas contains a moor corpse dating from the Iron Age (c 490BC). When first discovered in 1835 it was thought to be the body of a Viking queen, and Frederick VI paid for an expensive coffin. Another interesting feature of the church is that 23 skulls have been set into the masonry of the northern wall.

During the Middle Ages, **Kolding** (pop. 45,000, 310km/193 miles *see also* Route 7, *page 50*) was a border town between the duchy of Schleswig and the kingdom of Denmark, a role it relinquished in 1920 (*see page 13*). The town has some magnificent sights, including the ★★ **Trapholt Museum of Art**, with present-day design, furniture and crafts, and also ★★ **Koldinghus** with its cultural-historical exhibitions. Koldinghus burnt down in 1806; the oldest section of the building dates from the mid-15th century. Rebuilding is still taking place today, and the combination of the fortress's ancient substance with ultra-modern architecture is both unique and very successful. Plants from all over the world, organised according to their native geographical region, can be admired in the ★ **geographical garden**.

A detour now via the Daisy Route leads closer to the coast and to the Skamlingsbanken, the highest hill in southern Jutland (113m/370ft, superb view).

The main route continues directly to **Christiansfeld** (pop. 2,600), 325km (201 miles). The Danish Moravian Brethren, known as *Herrnhuter*, settled here in 1773, and their austere architecture is still much in evidence in the town (church, museum, herb garden, cemetery). Anyone with a sweet tooth will adore Christiansfeld's famous honey-cake.

★ **Haderslev** (pop. 20,000), 337km (209 miles), lies at the end of a narrow fjord which becomes a lake (Haderslev Dam, the biggest in southern Jutland) west of the town. The most impressive building in Haderslev is its Gothic **Vor Fruekirke**, often referred to as its cathedral, with its huge 16-m (52-ft) high windows in the choir. The cathedral is surrounded by some fine houses in the ★ **Old Town.**

The ★ **Haderslev Museum** contains archaeological relics as well as examples of rural dwellings in its open-air section. Old coaches can be admired in the Slesvigske Vognsamling, and ceramics and pottery in Louis Ehlers Lertøjssamling, housed inside the recently-restored half-timbered building at No 20 Slotsgade. No 25 is a very interesting mixture of a gallery, cinema, café-restaurant and live music venue.

Åbenrå (pop. 16,000, 361km/224 miles, *see also* Route 6, *page 48*) is the home of Denmark's only German daily newspaper, *Der Nordschleswiger*. The city centre has several picturesque corners in the area around the Vægterplads with its Night Watchman memorial. The Åbenrå Museum contains reminders of the time when the town was a major trading centre with its own fleet in the 17th and 18th centuries.

At the end of Route 4 is the border town of **Kruså** (*see also* Route 6, *page 47*), 386km (239 miles), with its many shops specialising in everything that's cheaper in Denmark than across the border (eg coffee, cheese, tea, candles, etc). The 'Heerweg' *(see page 48)* leads west from here and makes an interesting detour, and the former Nazi internment camp of **Frøslevejren** *(see page 47)* is also not far away.

Typical old town house in Haderslev

Night Watchman memorial

Ceramic collection, Haderslev Museum

Route 5

Århus

A summer visitor

The harbour town of Århus (pop. 165,000) on the east coast of Jutland is in many ways the opposite of Copenhagen, and is often referred to ironically by the Danes as 'the world's smallest city' (*verdens mindste Storby*). One of its greatest attractions is the beautiful natural scenery that surrounds it: there are forests to the north and south, more natural landscape around the Brabrandsø to the west, and to the east is Århus Bay, part of the Kattegat, with unspoilt beaches.

Århus was founded during Viking times. It became a bishopric in 948 and was granted its charter in 1441. The harbour, and railway construction in the middle of the 19th century contributed greatly to the size of Århus today. The

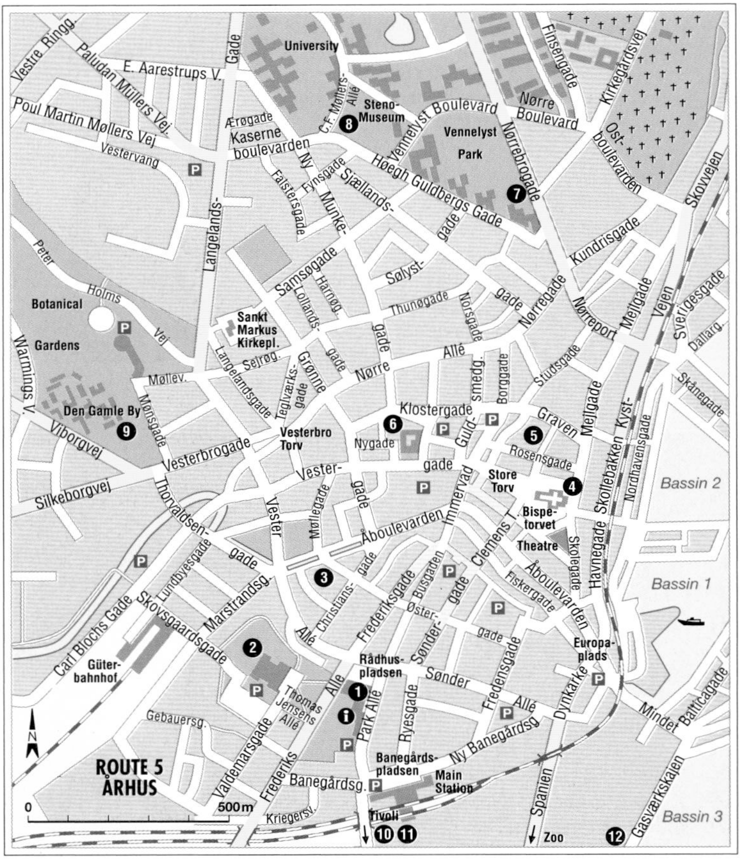

Inside Århus Cathedral

town is also reaping benefits from the gradual move towards decentralisation in Denmark.

The country's second-largest university is based here and there is a superb programme of cultural events: Århus has its own symphony orchestra and also an opera house, which is famous beyond the country's borders for its Wagner performances. Århus Festival Week (*see page 81*) is a magnet for culture lovers from all over Europe.

Sights

★ **Århus Town Hall** ❶ (Rådhuspladsen/Park Allé). This marble-faced steel-and-concrete structure, built between 1938 and 1941 by Arne Jakobsen (*see page 80*) and Erik Møller, is a good example of Danish Functionalism. There are two fountain sculptures here worthy of note: the first, *Agnete and the Water-Spirit,* stands near the entrance to the information office; the second is the playful *Pigs' Fountain* in front of the main entrance to the Town Hall. The glass facade of the **House of Music** (*Musikhuset*) ❷ (Thomas Jensens Allé; for ticket reservations tel: 86 13 43 44) lends the building a surprising lightness. Since its opening in 1982 the House of Music has been the centre of cultural life. Symphony concerts (September to June), opera performances and also guest performances by world-renowned artists are just part of the repertoire. Modern art in the foyer and the restaurant and café are extra attractions. The **Århus Arts Center** ❸ (JM Mørksgade 15) has exhibitions and also houses the **Poster Museum**, with its collection of several thousand posters from the past 120 years.

Town Hall interior

East of the Town Hall, it's not far to the sequence of streets known as the **Ryesgade-Søndergade-Clemens Torv**. Århus's shopping mile is often referred to as the city's *Strøget*, just like its opposite number in Copenhagen. At its southern end is the **railway station**, and at the northern end ★ **Århus Cathedral** ❹ (Bispetorv), consecrated

Relaxing on the Strøget

Wall decoration in the cathedral

to St Clement during the Catholic era. It is the longest church in Denmark (93m/305ft), and was built in the Flamboyant Gothic style between 1450 and 1520 on the site of an earlier Romanesque structure. The highlight inside is a gold ★ **altarpiece** (1479) by Lübeck master Bernt Notke, and the frescoes (c 1500).

Also in the area of the cathedral are the **Theatre** (Bispetorvet), a **Viking Museum**, in the basement of a bank (Clemens Torv), and also the only ★ **Women's Museum** (Domkirkeplads 5) in Europe, much of it documenting living and working conditions faced by women in the 19th and 20th centuries; exhibitions featuring the work of women artists are often held in the museum. In 1991 a casino opened in the **Hotel Royal** (Bispegade); it operates a strict dress code.

North of here is Århus's **Latin Quarter** (*Latinerkvarteret*) ❺, a lively, multi-cultural student area with lots of boutiques, cafés, pubs and restaurants. Not far to the west, via Lille Torv and the Vestergade, is the **Church of Our Lady** (*Vor Frue Kirke*) ❻ (Frue Kirkplads), which dates from the 13th century. Highlights inside include an ornate ★ **altarpiece** by Claus Berg (*see page 80*) and a richly ornamented crucifix dating from around 1400. During renovation work (1955–6) a previous three-aisled structure was discovered beneath the crypt; since then it has been restored and reconsecrated, and is now known as the ★ **Crypt of St Nicholas** (*Sankt Nikolai Kryptkirke*).

Around 0.5km (¼ mile) north of here is the **Vennelyst Park**, with the ★ **Århus Museum of Art** ❼ at its southeastern corner. It has a fine collection of 18th- and 19th-century Danish painting and sculpture, a fascinating display of runic stones, and is considered one of the leading museums for modern Danish art (several works by Per Kirkeby are on display). The exterior of the museum matches that of the university buildings in the nearby **University Park** (*Universitetspark*); built between 1932 and 1941 in Danish 'Brick Functionalist' style, they form a harmonious ensemble. The park also contains the **Natural History Museum**, with exhibitions documenting the fauna and flora of Denmark; and a new building opened at the beginning of 1994 houses the **Steno Museum** ❽ (CF Møllers Allé 2), a science museum with lots of hands-on exhibits devoted to themes of natural science, medicine and astronomy.

'The Old Town', and visitors

Southwest of here is the spacious **Botanical Garden** (Peter Holms Vej) and the open-air museum known as ★★ **The Old Town** (*Den Gamle By*) ❾ (Eugen Warmings Vej/Viborgvej), which documents town life from the 16th to the 19th centuries. Around 70 houses from all over Denmark have been brought here. The many workshops are very interesting, as are the special collections of toys, clocks, etc. Opera performances staged in the old theatre of Helsingør, built there in 1817 and then moved to its present location in the Old Town in 1961, are an experience not to be missed.

South of the centre, Århus has several more sights nestling in a marvellous park and forest landscape. At the northern edge of this green area is the pleasure park of **Tivoli-Friheden** ❿ (Skovbrynet). Not far away is **Marselisborg Castle** ⓫ (Kongevejen 100), built between 1899 and 1902, the summer residence of the Danish royal family. Public access to the park is permitted providing no member of the royal family is staying at the castle. If the queen is at home, the changing of the guard can be observed daily around noon.

Changing of the castle guard

Below the castle in the direction of the bay, a memorial (Mindepark) commemorates Danes from southern Jutland who died after being conscripted into the German army during World War I.

Further inland from the castle is a **botanical garden** and, further south, a **zoo** (*Dyrehaven*). The **Marselisborg Forest** extends a full 10km (6 miles) along the coast here. Those following the Daisy Route (*see page 40*) will find excellent hiking routes, beaches, a campsite, pubs and also the ★★ **Moesgård Prehistoric Museum** ⓬ (Moesgård Allé 20, 8270 Hojbjerg). The exhibits give a good general impression of the Stone, Bronze, Iron and Viking ages. The museum's most treasured possession is the well-preserved 2,000-year-old body of the ★★ **Grauballe Man**, found in the moor in 1952. A 4-km (2-mile) long information route leads from the museum to the sea and back again, passing prehistoric houses and burial sites.

Prehistoric Museum: Alphabet Stone

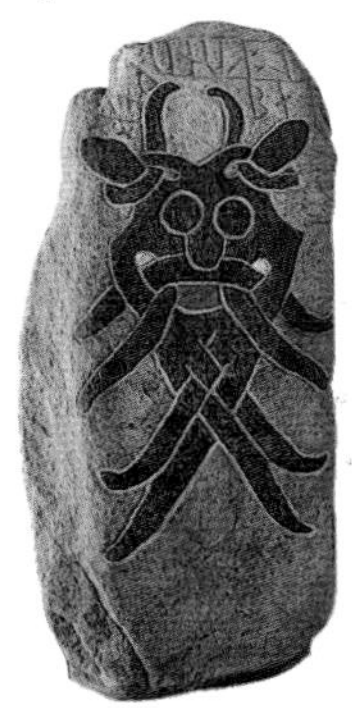

For more excursions in the region see Route 4, *page 37* and Route 8, *page 52*.

World War I memorial

Route 6

Around Southern Jutland: Rømø – Højer – Tønder – Kruså – Sønderborg – Als – Åbenrå – Løgumkloster – Rømø (200km/124 miles)

This route leads across the border region with Germany, where a by no means peaceful history has left a number of traces and scars.

One of Rømø's famous beaches

The starting point for this round trip is **Rømø** (pop. 840, 12,886ha/31,841 acres), Denmark's largest North Sea island, with the broadest ★ beaches in Europe. There is a road to the beach near Lakolk (surf areas marked), much of which is open to cars.

The magnificent, three-winged mansion of ★ **Kommandørgård** (1746) at Toftum in the north of the island is a reminder of the town's heyday in the 17th and 18th century, when men from Rømø grew rich on whaling ships off the Greenland coast. The early 13th-century Rømø Kirke in Kirkeby with its fine votive ships, and the neighbouring churchyard with ★ **tomb slabs** of Greenland whaling captains on its northern wall also reflect just how important the industry was. The Rømø Sommerland Recreation Park in Havneby is ideal for children.

In memory of a whaler

Leave Rømø now along the 9-km (5-mile) long Rømødamm (1939–48), turn south at the mainland and then follow the 419 to **Højer** (pop. 1,500, 24km/14 miles). Towering above this town with all its listed buildings is the largest windmill in Denmark (open in summer with exhibitions on marshland and mud-flats).

The dykes and sluices at the ★★ **mud-flats** further west are also interesting. An old fishing community has been revived near the Højer Sluse (1861) on the banks of the Videå. The information centre near the modern ★ **Vidå**

Sluse provides a lot of interesting facts about the unique yet very sensitive natural environment here. The ★★ mudflats dry out twice a day at low tide and are then flooded again at high tide. This ecological system is essential to the survival of many different kinds of flora and fauna.

The next destination on the route is **Mageltønder**, 31km (19 miles). The ★ Slotsgade, lined with lime-trees and picturesque Frisian houses (most of them 18th-century) connects the ornate and originally ★ Romanesque church with the baroque palace of Schackenborg. It is the property of Prince Joachim, second in line to the Danish throne.

Mageltønder's Romanesque church

Travel to **Tønder** (*see* Route 2, *page 29*), 36km (22 miles), and on to Tinglev, 60km (37 miles). Near Fårhus, 70km (43 miles), a side-road leads through the forest of Frøslev to the former Nazi internment camp of ★ **Frøslevejren**. Many members of the Danish Resistance passed through here on their way to concentration camps. Exhibitions in the huts document camp life.

Frøslevejren camp

Take road number 8 now to **Kruså**, 75km (46 miles). An alternative route at this point is the attractive coast road known as *Fjordvejen* which begins on the other side of Kruså; it travels along the Flensburger Förde and meets the main route again near Rinkenæs, 87km (54 miles). North of Egernsund, 90km (55 miles), is **Gråsten Palace**, built on the remains of an even more magnificent palace that was destroyed by fire in 1757; the ★ **baroque church** (1699), however, escaped the flames (open in summer on certain days of the week when the palace is not occupied). Gråsten Palace is the home of the Queen Mother.

The town of **Dybbøl** (pop. 2,000, 100km/62 miles), is closely bound up with Danish–German relations: in 1864 Danish troops fended off five times as many Prussians in a defensive battle on the fortifications that lasted 34 days, before they were finally overrun on 18 April and southern Jutland was lost for 56 years (*see pages 12–13,*

A street in Tønder

Dybbøl Mill

1864 and 1920). ★ **Dybbøl Mill**, which lay at the centre of the Danish positions, is today a national monument.

★ **Sønderborg** (pop. 25,000), 105km (65 miles), extends along both sides of the southern entrance to the Als Sund, which is guarded by ★ **Sønderborg Castle**, state property since the 1920 reunification. The castle contains a museum documenting the history and culture of southern Jutland. The four-winged brick building underwent major renovation in the 18th century, when its exterior was renovated in the baroque style. Parts of the interior, eg the castle chapel dating from 1570, have Renaissance features. The town itself is particularly pretty down by the harbour.

Sønderborg harbour

Sønderborg lies on the island of **Als** (pop. 51,000, 31,220ha/77,146 acres), a popular resort island with many campsites and holiday homes, but also home to one of the country's biggest industrial firms, Danfoss, well-known for its heating technology. Road number 8 travels right across Als to the ferry port of Fynshav with connections to Bøjden on Fyn (seven or eight departures daily, *see also* Route 9, *page 55*).

From Mommark it's possible in summer to take a ferry to the island of Ærø (*see page 61*). Halfway between the two harbours, in the small forest of Blomeskobbel, are four prehistoric tombs (long and round dolmens). The rococo Augustenborg Palace (1776) and also Nordborg Palace, which was renovated during the 1920s, are both impressive structures, but unfortunately closed to the public.

Route 6 leads from Sønderborg via **Åbenrå** (136km/84 miles, *see also* Route 4, *page 41*) to Rødekro and then joins the 429. At the level crossing in Rødekro, 144km (89 miles), the route crosses the **Heerweg**, the most important connecting route between Northern and Central Europe for millenia until the advent of the railway. It was used by pilgrims, warriors and traders but especially by cattle dealers. The old route is no longer preserved in its entirety, but there are still several fascinating details: the old Urnehobved thingstead up at Bolderslev, for instance, or bridges such as the Immervad Bro (1776), north of Rødekro, and the Pouls Bro near the former pilgrimage destination of Kliplev (★ 13th-century church) to the south.

Løgumkloster church interior

Løgumkloster (pop. 3,000), 169km (105 miles), developed around an important Cistercian monastery, the ★ brick church of which is a good example of the transition from Romanesque to Gothic. Unfortunately the church is almost all that remains of the original monastery. Southwest of here on the way to Tønder it's possible to hike through ★ **Draved Skov**, Denmark's last primeval forest. Then it's back to the island of **Rømø** (200km/124 miles) via Skærbæk (pop. 3,000), 186km (115 miles), and the Rømødamm.

Route 7

Through South Central Jutland: Esbjerg – Egtved – Kolding – Fredericia – Vejle – Jelling – Billund – Esbjerg (225km/140 miles)

This route leads from the southern North Sea coast to the Little Belt and back again, taking in both ancient and modern sights, including the ever-popular Legoland.

Esbjerg (pop. 72,000) is the fifth-largest town in Denmark. As well as being essential to the Danish oil and gas industry as a land base, it is the first port of call for visitors arriving by ferry from Harwich in the UK. The harbour is also home to an important fishing fleet. ★ Fish auctions are held at 7am, Monday to Friday.

Esbjerg fishing fleet

The ★ **Horns Rev Fireship**, near the docks of the Fanø ferry, is at permanent anchor as a floating museum. The ★★ **Fishery and Seafaring Museum and Salt-Water Aquarium** is full of fascinating exhibits. It also has a sealarium, where seals can be observed through glass. Esbjerg was created for a very practical reason: after the loss of Schleswig and Holstein (*see page 12*) and the North Sea harbour there, the decision was made to build the harbour at Esbjerg, and the town flourished as a result. The architecture thus reflects the neoclassical trend of that time, and there are many late 19th-century versions of Gothic, Renaissance, baroque, etc. The Esbjerg Museum documents the history of the town and region, and also possesses a remarkable collection of emeralds. The ★ **Esbjerg Art Museum** is particularly good on Surrealism and Constructivism, but the town's latest artistic acquisition is right on the beach: the four ★ **giant sculptures** 'Menesker ved Hovet' by Swend Hansen.

Traditional Fanø costumes

People don't normally stay too long in Esbjerg, though, preferring the island offshore known as ★ **Fanø** (pop. 3,200, 5,578ha/13,783 acres). It has broad ★ **sandy beaches** (there's a nudist beach near Fanø Bad, with a surfing

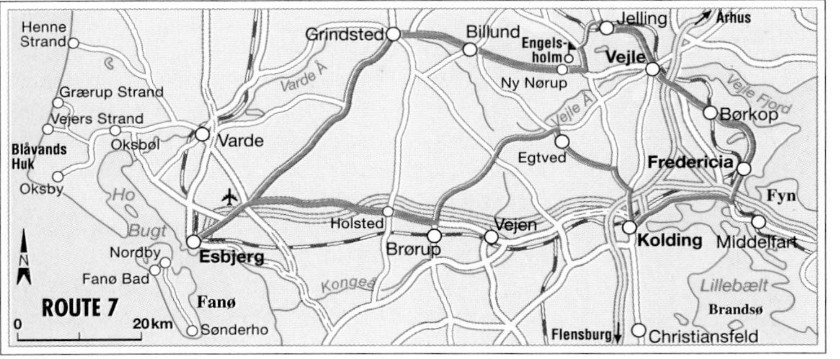

The Hannes Hus in Sønderho

Thatching a roof

beach in the middle) and an unspoilt area of forests and sand-dunes with many footpaths. The island villages of **Nordby** to the north and the smaller ★ **Sønderho** to the south of the island, with their numerous thatched houses, are idyllic. **Fanø Bad**, right on the North Sea coast, has a long tradition as a beach resort, but has been somewhat disfigured by apartment hotels. The museums and collections here include the Fanø Shipping and Folkwear Collection, the ★ **Fanø Museum** (both in Nordby) and also **Hannes Hus** in Sønderho, all of them documenting the time when the island was famous for its shipyards and trading fleet (18th and 19th century). The island churches in Sønderho are like miniature model-ship museums (14 votive ships in Sønderho, 9 in Nordby).

The coastal region north of Esbjerg around Blåvands Huk (marked by a square lighthouse) is equally popular with holidaymakers. Holiday home and campsite communities such as Blåvand, Oksby, Vejers Strand, Grærup Strand and Børsmose Strand receive a lot of visitors in summer, especially Germans. In between are training zones for the Danish army (observe warning signs) and German bunkers dating from World War II (Bunker Museum Tirpitz-Stellung). The Refugees' Cemetery next to the church in Oksbøl testifies to the horrors of the Third Reich. At the end of the war around 40,000 refugees from the east were living together in one camp (there is also an Oksbøl Museum). The former camp hospital is in use today as a youth hostel.

From Esbjerg, Route 7 now follows the E20, but then switches just before Brørup, 39km (24 miles), to the much quieter 417, and then carries on northwards to **Egtved** (pop. 1,900), 62km (38 miles), famous as the place where the *Girl of Egtved* was found. The young girl was buried in a mound inside an oak coffin around 3,000 years ago, and her remains, clothing and coffin, discovered in 1921, are still in excellent condition. A miniature museum at the spot shows copies of the finds (the originals are in the Copenhagen National Museum, *see page 20*).

Further to the north, along the edge of the picturesque ★ **Vejle Aa Valley** (*Vejle Ådal*), with its fine cycle and hiking routes, the artist Robert Jacobsen (*see page 80*) and his French apprentice Jean Clareboudt have transformed the old ★★ **Tørskind Grusgrav** gravel pit into an impressive *Gesamtkunstwerk* with the aid of nine massive landscape sculptures made of wood, steel, stone and concrete.

The route continues eastwards now via Kolding, 81km (50 miles, *see page 40*) to the Little Belt, the stretch of water separating Fyn and Jutland. It is spanned by two striking bridges: a 1,177-m (3,861-ft) long steel construction (1935) and a 1,700-m (5,570-ft) long motorway bridge, built in 1970. (Crossing to Fyn: Route 9, *see page 55*, or Route 11, *see page 68.*)

Fredericia (pop. 28,000, 107km/66 miles), began as a fortified town around 1650. The centre is surrounded by ramparts and laid out in the grid pattern that was popular during the Renaissance. Shortly after its foundation Fredericia received several privileges, including freedom of religion. This meant that Catholics, Jews and Huguenots were drawn to the town. The Fredericia Museum documents the history of the town's fortress (used for military purposes until 1909). The Trinity Church contains a fine collection of ★ baroque furniture.

Route 7 now leaves Fredericia to the north in the direction of Vejle (Route 4, *page 40*), 130km (80 miles). From Børkop it's possible to follow the Daisy Route, which leads across the beautiful landscape of the ★ **Munkebjerg** and along the bank of the Vejle Fjord into the town. From Vejle continue along the Daisy Route as far as ★ **Jelling** (pop. 2,100, 141km/87 miles). This town is considered the cradle of the Kingdom of Denmark (*see page 11*, 950), as documented on the ★★ **rune stones** outside the Romanesque church. When the more northern of the two artificial mounds next to the church was excavated, it was found that the burial chambers were empty. King Gorm (*see page 11;* 950) and his wife Thyra were probably buried here before their son Harald Bluetooth was converted to Christianity and had them moved inside the church; Gorm's mortal remains were discovered under the choir in 1978. The frescoes inside are the result of some 'restoration' work on the Romanesque originals.

On the way to Billund, a visit to Engelsholm Castle north of Ny Nørup can easily be included. This one-wing building (now an adult education centre) with a mighty tower at each end was renovated in the baroque style in the 18th century; there is public access to the park outside the ramparts.

The big attraction in **Billund** (pop. 5,200, 165km/102 miles), is guaranteed to delight children: ★★ **Legoland Park**, a world made up entirely of millions of pieces of LEGO, as well as a ★ doll museum, the miniature ★ **Titania's Palace**, a Wild West town, a driving school for children, etc. The outside area is open from May until mid-September, and the interior exhibitions until just before Christmas. The LEGO firm began in a joiner's workshop in Billund in the 1930s; most of it is still owned by the family that founded it. Near the park, the ★ Center Mobilium contains three technical museums in one (rescue services, air travel and cars).

When it arrives at Grindsted, 175km (108 miles), Route 7 turns into road number 30, which leads back to the starting point of the route, **Esbjerg**, 225km (139 miles).

Trinity Church interior

Rune Stones

Engelsholm Castle

LEGO Mt Rushmore

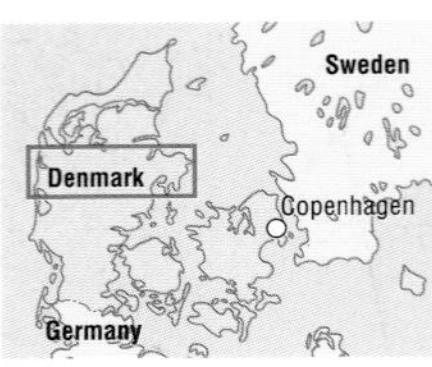

Route 8

Across North Central Jutland: Søndervig – Ringkøbing – Herning – Silkeborg – Viborg – Århus – Ebeltoft – Grenå (200km/124 miles)

This route covers a variety of scenery, from the moors of Central Jutland to the lake-strewn high country, and on to the picturesque Djursland Peninsula.

The Gothic church tower in Ringkøbing

The route runs from the North Sea resort of **Søndervig** *(see also* Route 2, *page 30*) along the northern bank of the Ringkøbing Fjord. Shortly before you get to the town there is the Romanesque ★ Gammel Sogn Kirke with its frescoes dating from 1170.

★ **Ringkøbing** (pop. 8,700, 9km/5 miles), is the main shopping town in this coastal area, and is a lively place. The local information office has pamphlets detailing recommended tours of the town, its attractive old section in particular. In summer it is also possible to follow the night watchmen doing their rounds. The reason that the tower of the Gothic brick church (1550) beside the market square looks slightly bent is because it gets wider as it gets higher.

Hee, a few kilometres further on, contains an important Roman square-stoned church, and also the popular **Sommerland West** amusement park, ideal for children. The modest-looking **Ølstrup Kirke** (18km/11 miles, north of road number 15) contains an ★ altarpiece by the German expressionist painter Emil Nolde.

Herning (pop. 29,000, 55km/34 miles), only had 20 inhabitants in 1840, but it grew into a busy town with an exhibition centre. The patronage of the local textile industry has since turned the town of Herning into an important centre of the arts.

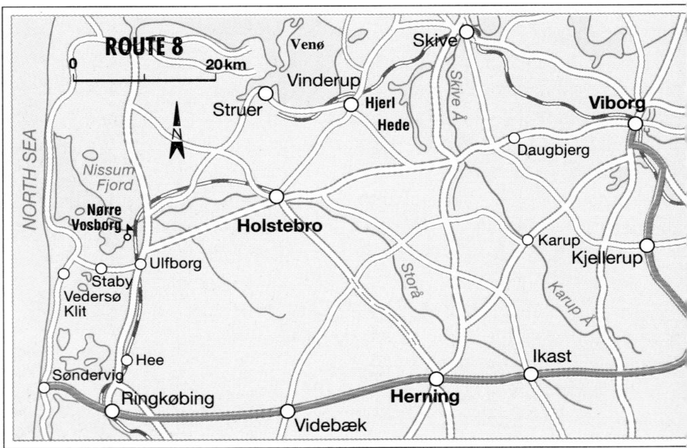

A complex of buildings here in the suburb of Birk (directly on Route 8) should not be missed. The ★ **Herning Art Museum** *(Kunstmuseen)* contains an exquisite collection of Danish and international art, concentrating on work done since the 1960s (Vasserely, Manzoni, etc). The inner courtyard of the spiral-shaped building is adorned by a 220-m (720-ft) long ★ **ceramic frieze** by Carl-Henning Pedersen. Next door, the ★ **Carl-Henning Pedersen and Else Alfelt Museum**, housed in two architecturally remarkable buildings (also with ceramics), is devoted exclusively to works by the famous artist and his wife. The round building dates from 1976, and the pyramid from 1993. A small wood behind the building contains a sculpture park.

Enjoying a rest

In the centre of Herning, the Denmark Photographic Museum documents the history of photographic art, and the Herning Museum contains local folklore exhibitions.

Route 8 continues via Ikast, 67km (41 miles), leaving the flat moors of central Jutland for the more varied landscape of the high country, with its forests and lakes, all lined up along Denmark's longest river, the Gudenå. This region is a paradise for hikers and cyclists (there are marked routes of varying lengths), and also for canoeists, but the latter are having to cope with various environmental restrictions (contact local information offices for more details).

Silkeborg Museum of Art

The main town in the area is ★ **Silkeborg** (pop. 36,000, 95km/59 miles), situated beside a lake. Its latest attraction is ★ **Aqua**, a freshwater museum. The town has two more excellent museums. The ★★ **Silkeborg Museum of Art** developed from the collection of the artist Asger Jorn (*see page 80*). Jorn wanted to document the origins and development of abstract-spontaneous art, and his own works (★★ *Stalingrad*) and those by contemporaries that he col-

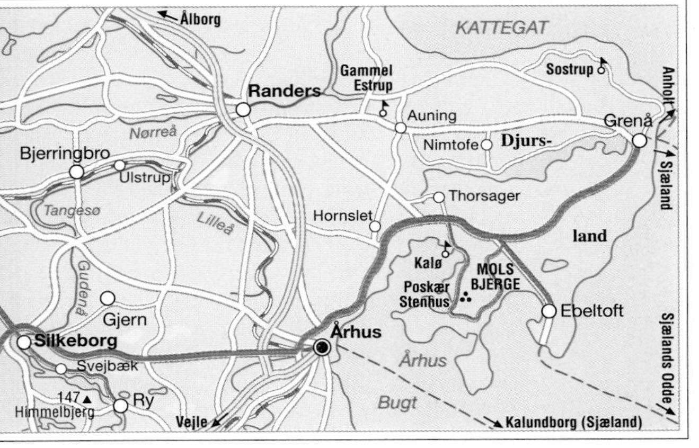

The Man of Tollund

Family day out at Himmelbjerg

lected – including graphics and ceramics – form a fascinating collection.

The other museum is the ★ **Silkeborg Museum**, whose highlights include the ★★ Iron Age Exhibition, based around the 2,200-year-old corpse of ★★ **The Man of Tollund**, discovered on the moors in 1950.

There's one way of discovering the region around Silkeborg that's hard to resist: taking a trip on the ★ **Hjejlen paddle-steamer**, which has been in continuous service since 1861. It also docks at the foot of the 147-m (480-ft) high ★★ **Himmelbjerg**, thought to be the highest peak in Denmark until the mid-19th century. The view across the lake-strewn landscape from up here is utterly breathtaking. The tower at the summit is a memorial to Frederick VII and the constitution he signed in 1849, and there are several other monuments to national events in the immediate area. One sight worth visiting nearby is the ★ **Jutland Automobile Museum** in Gjern, north of Silkeborg. The oldest car is a Belgian one dating from 1900.

From Silkeborg, it is worth taking a detour northwards to the town of **Viborg**, whose historical importance stems from its position at the northern end of the Heerweg (*see page 48*). Although the **cathedral** was founded in 1130, the present building was founded only in 1876. Nevertheless it has some beautiful fresoes by Joakim Skovgård. The museum next door is dedicated to Skovgård and other artists, while **Viborg Museum** has workshops and products of the town's craftsmen.

Route 8 continues through **Århus**, the second-largest city in Denmark (133km/82 miles, *see* Route 5, *page 42*), and on to the **Djursland Peninsula** with its varied landscape made up of wooded hills, moors and beaches. Impressive prehistoric monuments (dolmens and burial chambers) can be found in many places. The most impressive relic, the stone-age **Poskær Stenhus** lies in the picturesque, wooded ★ **Mols Bjerge**, along the road from Agri to Grønfeld.

Just below the Mols Bjerge, in the south of the peninsula, is the immaculate town of ★ **Ebeltoft**, with the bright flowers of Raadhusgarden echoing the tiles of the Gamle Radhus, the smallest town hall in Denmark built in 1789. There are old streets, cobbled houses and even a night watch, to see that all is well. The pride of the harbour is the restored frigate *Jylland*, the last of a line of famous wooden battleships.

It is impossible to go further east in Jutland than **Grenå** (pop. 14,000, 200km/124 miles). As regional capital, it is home to the Djursland Museum. Right on the harbour is the modern ★ **Kattegatcenter**, an aquarium complex displaying the full diversity of Denmark's marine life, as well as some sharks imported from warmer waters.

Route 9

Route 9A – Across Fyn: Middelfart – Odense – Nyborg (73km/45 miles)

Route 9B – Around Fyn: Middelfart – Assens – Fåborg – Svendborg – Tåsinge – Langeland – Nyborg – Kerteminde – Odense – Bogense – Middelfart (240km/150 miles)

Route 9C – The Island of Ærø

Fyn, the 'Garden of Denmark', has always had excellent soil, and people have lived well here since prehistoric times. No other part of the country has such superb old

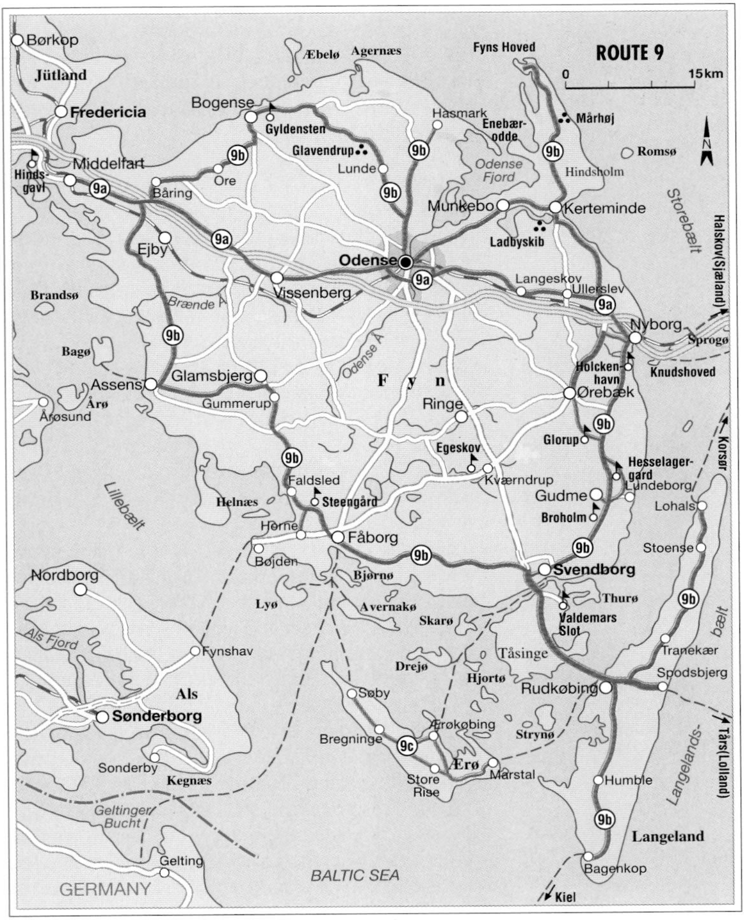

Egeskov Manor, inside and out

castles and manor houses in such numbers: all the architectural styles are in evidence, from the Romanesque Nyborg Castle to the neoclassical Holstenhuus mansion near Fåborg, which was built in 1910.

★★ **Egeskov Manor** near Kværndrup, between Odense (Route 9A) and Svendborg (Route 9B), in a fairytale setting in the middle of a lake, is one of Europe's most attractive Renaissance manor houses, and should definitely be visited. The great hall inside is very impressive, and is now used for concerts. The 15-ha (37-acre) park in which it is set is just as magnificent, with fuchsia bushes and clipped box-tree hedges, a bamboo maze and an ancient herb garden. There are exhibitions of coaches and agricultural implements in the outhouses, and also a vintage car museum.

Routes 9A and 9B across Fyn both begin in Middelfart and can be connected with Route 11 (*beginning on page 65*) at the Little Belt. Driving straight across Fyn (78km/48 miles) can be done in 45 minutes via the E20 motorway. Route 9A travels along the parallel roads numbered 161 and 160.

Route 9A

Middelfart (pop. 12,500) actually means middle crossing, because of its geographical position at the centre of the Little Belt. The town's role as a bridgehead is documented in the ★ **Middelfart Museum**, inside the Henner Früsers Hus, a half-timbered structure dating from 1570. There are also exhibitions on the subject of whaling: until the end of the 19th century the Little Belt was the most important whaling centre in Denmark; inside the Church of St Nicholas the massive jawbone of a whale caught in 1603 can be seen hanging on a wall.

To the west of Middelfart, near the old Lillbælt Bridge (road number 161), is a fine stretch of forest with attractive hiking paths.

Fun at Fyns Sommerland

Along the 161 between Middelfart and Odense there are several more attractions, including the ★ **Fyns Sommerland** amusement park for children, 21km (13 miles), and all manner of animals to be observed around the village of Vissenberg, 28km (17 miles), at the Fyns Aquarium, the Vissenberg Terrarium and, a bit further south, the Frydenlund Bird Park.

Nyborg Slot

Now the decision has to be made whether to take the 161 to the centre of **Odense** (*see page 62*), or to drive around the city along its southern ring road. To the east of Odense, road number 160 leads via Langeskov and Ullerslev (62km/38 miles, antiques on sale at Hindemae mansion), to ★ **Nyborg** (pop. 15,000, 73km/45 miles). The main attraction here is the oldest royal castle in Denmark: the Romanesque ★★ **Nyborg Slot**, built around

Vestlyns Hjemstavnsgård museum

1170 and centre of the Kingdom of Denmark for almost 200 years. The town also has several other fine historic sights, including the ★ longest town gate (40m/130ft) in the country *(Landporten)*, and the mayor's courtyard *(Mads Lerches Gaard)* with its half-timbered houses, containing a folklore museum.

Houses in the mayor's courtyard

To the east of Nyborg are the Knudshovet ferry docks, from where passengers used to embark for the crossing across the Storebælt (Great Belt) to Halskov on Sjælland. Now the jouney can be made by rail or road across the spectacular ★★ **Great Belt Fixed Link**, which came into operation in 1998. Spanning a total of 18km (11 miles) via the island of Sprogø, the link comprises the West Bridge for cars and trains (at 6.6km Europe's longest combined road and rail bridge); the East Bridge for cars (at 6.8km the world's second largest suspension bridge); and the 8-km long East Tunnel for trains). It is the largest construction project ever undertaken in Denmark.

Route 9B

The best scenery is along the Daisy Route out of Middelfart and then along road number 313 to **Assens** (pop. 5,600), 35km (21 miles), birthplace of the seafaring hero Peter Willemoes (1783–1808), who is famous for his role at the Battle of Copenhagen (memorial at the harbour, memorial museum in his birthplace). The private Ernst Collection of porcelain, glass and silver is also worth a visit. Southeast of the town, amateur gardeners can draw much inspiration from seven gardens inspired by different countries *(De 7 Haver)*.

Beyond Glamsbjerg turn off to the south and drive via Gummerup (52km/32 miles; very good folklore museum at ★ **Vestlyns Hjemstavnsgård**, inside one of Fyn's finest half-timbered courtyards), to Falsled, a small village right next to the sea.

De 7 Haver gardens

South of Steensgaard, on the Horne Land peninsula, is the ★ **Horne Kirke**, the only Romanesque round church on Fyn, which received a nave in Gothic times and also a mighty west front; it looks somewhat odd as a result. The interior includes an unusual 'count's balcony' (1820), based on theatre boxes in Copenhagen. The ferry port of Bøjden, 6km (3¾ miles) west of here, connects regularly with Fynshav on Als (*see* Route 6, *page 48*).

★ **Fåborg** (pop. 7,200, 75km/46 miles), has several picturesque corners in its old town, and they can be admired from the bell tower of the now-demolished Church of St Nicholas. There are works by the Fyn Painters (*see page 80*) and also local sculptors including Kai Nielsen (1882–1924) in the ★ **Fåborg Museum for Fyns Malerkunst**, which is housed in a fine neoclassical building (1905). Kai Nielsen was also responsible for the fountain in the market square.

★ **Svendborg** (pop. 26,000), 100km (62 miles), is the second-largest town on Fyn. There are some well-restored half-timbered houses in the centre and granaries at the harbour. The busy pedestrian precincts, with their cafés, pubs and restaurants, are definitely worth exploring. Anne Hvides Gård (1560) is a museum of culture and history (18th–19th century), and ★ **Viebæltegård** (almshouses in use until 1974) contains several exhibitions including many archaeological finds from the area. Fauna from all over Denmark, especially birds, can be admired at the slide-shows held in ★ **Svendborg's Zoological Museum**. There are also enjoyable ferry trips to be had locally, to the beautiful little islands of **Hjortø**, **Skarø** and ★ **Drejø**, or in the summer to ★ Tåsinge on the ★ ***MS Helge***, a vintage ship (1924).

Sailing between the islands

South of Svendborg, across the Svendborgsund Bridge, is the island of ★ **Tåsinge** (pop. 6,000, 6,979ha/17,245

Fertile farmland

acres). The highlight here is the baroque ★★ **Valdemars Slot** with its manor museum. Froense, the main town on Tåsinge, has several idyllic, thatched, half-timbered buildings; one of them housing the ★ Seafaring Museum.

★★ **Langeland** (pop. 15,157, 21,381ha/52,833 acres) not only has flat beaches that are ideal for children but also several rocky stretches of coastline, especially in the south and in the vicinity of Ristinge, where Langeland points across in the direction of Ærø. ★ **Rudkøbing**, the island's capital, has a very charming harbour and many picturesque little streets, particularly around the market square with a monument to the town's most famous son, the physicist HC Ørsted, who invented electromagnetism. There is a fine half-timbered courtyard just off the Østergade pedestrian precinct; today it contains the fascinating ★ Tingstedet antiques shop, complete with café.

Langeland has safe, sandy beaches

★ **Tranekær** is more of a village, and the north wing of the ★ **Tranekær Slot** dates from the 13th century. This castle has been the seat of the feudal counts of Ahlefeldt since 1672. The castle mill contains a museum. Langeland is very much a mill island: alongside several modern windmills used for generating electricity are 10 old ones, nine of which date from the last century. There are also around 30 known Stone Age burial chambers, including the one outside the unusually large Late Romanesque church in Humble: **Kong Humbles Grav**, a long dolmen measuring 55m x 9m (180ft x 29ft). The nearby mansion of Skovsgård contains a coach and cart museum, and also has a forestry exhibition.

Modern windmills

One very pleasant cultural surprise here in the Danish provinces is the highly-regarded series of ★ **classical music concerts**, held in Stoense Church in the north of Langeland in the summer.

The main route now leaves Svendborg in the direction of Nyborg. At Broholm mansion (112km/69 miles; Renaissance building dating from 1642), a road branches off towards Gudme, where recent excavations have uncovered the foundations of a large farm dating back to prehistoric migrations; the inhabitants of Gudme are eager to regard it as the centre of a prehistoric kingdom more ancient than Jelling (*see page 11,* 950).

Archaeologists have discovered the remains of an important port from the same era, on the coast, around the idyllic harbour community of ★ **Lundeborg**. A few kilometres farther north is the mansion of ★ **Hesselagergård**, a Renaissance building with unusual, Venetian-style round gables. One remnant of the Ice Age is Denmark's largest erratic boulder, the ★ **Dammestennen** (46m/150ft circumference). The main route leads straight to the Renaissance manor of ★ **Holckenhavn** (park open to the public) and past it to Nyborg (133km/82 miles; *see* Route 9A, *page*

56). An alternative here is to travel along part of the Daisy Route: past the baroque manor house of **Glorup** (16th–18th century; ★ huge park with sculptures) and on to Ørebæk, where the seven Stone Age ★★ **Lindeskov Graves** (burial chamber, round dolmen and long dolmen, one of them the longest in Denmark) lie in a wood to the west of the main road. Finally this route also reaches Nyborg.

Half-timbered heritage

From here Route 9B leads to the north of Fyn, past the half-timbered mansion of Risinge (built in 1730; central tower dates from 1903) to ★ **Kerteminde** (pop. 5,400), 153km (95 miles). This fishing town, which is home to a modern marine biology research centre, extends across the mouth of the Kerteminde Fjord and out towards the Baltic. There are several fine, half-timbered houses in the centre, and the folklore museum is inside the Farvergården (1630). Near the road that leaves the town heading north, the restored windmill of Svanemøllen points the way to the ★ Johannes Larsen Museum, where the famous landscape painter (1867–1961) lived and worked. Today his works are on display here along with several others by Fyn artists (*see page 80*).

Travelling north from Kerteminde, the peninsula of ★★ Hindsholm soon comes into view; it ends up in the nature protection area of ★ **Fyns Hoved** (22km/13 miles), one of the most varied stretches of coastal landscape in Denmark. Roughly 7km (4 miles) before the end of this cul-de-sac, on the east side of the road, lies Denmark's largest burial chamber ★ **Mårhoj** (take a torch).

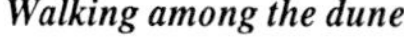
Walking among the dunes

Another mound to the southwest of Kerteminde formerly concealed the only burial ship of a Viking chieftain ever found in Denmark, the ★★ **Ladbyskib**. The hull of the 21-m (68-ft) long ship had rotted, but an excellent impression had been left in the soil, clearly showing the skeletons of 11 horses and four dogs, along with several iron nails and an anchor. Above the archaeological site is a miniature museum, shaped like a burial mound.

Decorative door knocker

The main route now continues from Kerteminde via the shipyard town of Munkebo to **Odense** (*see page 62*), 173km (107 miles), leaving the city again on the 162 along the harbour, and then switching to the 327. Northwest of Lunde, 185km (114 miles), a memorial grove called Glavendruplunden surrounds the ★ Glavendrup ship monument (*see page 79*). The ★★ **rune stone** dating from the Viking era with the longest known inscription in the country (over 200 symbols) forms the heart of it.

Nature lovers should consider making a detour at this point to the Enebærodde peninsula (conservation area, long hiking paths) at the mouth of the Odense Fjord. One of the finest beaches on Fyn extends across to the west from here as far as Flyvesand Point (dune area) on the Agernæs peninsula.

Passing the Renaissance manor of Gyldensteen, Route 9B arrives at **Bogense** (pop. 3,000, 208km/129 miles), the smallest town on Fyn. The town centre around the Adelgade, the Østergade and the church square *(Torvet)* is very picturesque. The highlight here since 1934 has been a *Manneken Pis* (a copy of the famous one in Brussels), opposite the information office.

Not far away to the southwest is Dorf Ore, 217km (134 miles), with the **Danmarks Husdyrpark**, a home for domestic pets. Near Båring, road number 317 meets up with the E20 and the 161; westwards it's not far to Middelfart, 240km (150 miles), the starting point of the journey.

Copy of Manneken Pis

Café in Aerøskøbing

Route 9C

★★ **Ærø** (pop. 7,800), an island measuring about 30km (18 miles) by 8km (5 miles), rounds off the southwestern corner of Fyn's 'Caribbean'. Small villages with thatched roofs and two charming towns add to the idyllic aspect of this enchanting island. The prettiest town is probably ★★ **Ærøskøbing** with winding streets, rose-covered thatched houses, colourful doorways and two ancient water-pumps in the market square, as well as the **Dukkehuset**, the smallest house in town. The most famous of the local museums here is the ★★ **bottled ship collection**.

★ **Marstal** seems a bit more modern, although it too experienced a heyday in the 18th and 19th centuries as a seafaring town; indeed, the merchant fleet here was larger than that of Copenhagen at one stage. Seafaring traditions live on in the ★ **Jens Hansen Seafaring Museum**.

Other sights on Ærø include country churches and prehistoric structures: Bregninge Kirke has Late Gothic frescoes and an ★ altar by Claus Berg *(see page 80)*. There are remains of some ramparts dating from Viking times at Søby Voldanlæg, and next to the village church in Store Rise is a dolmen grave dating from 3000BC.

Clipper in Marstal Harbour

Route 10

Odense

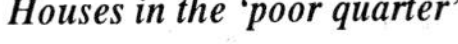

Houses in the 'poor quarter'

The university town of Odense (pop. 180,000), birthplace of Hans Christian Andersen, lies at the centre of the island of Fyn. Efficient transport connections, good hotels and a wide range of cultural attractions make Odense an ideal base from which to explore the whole island.

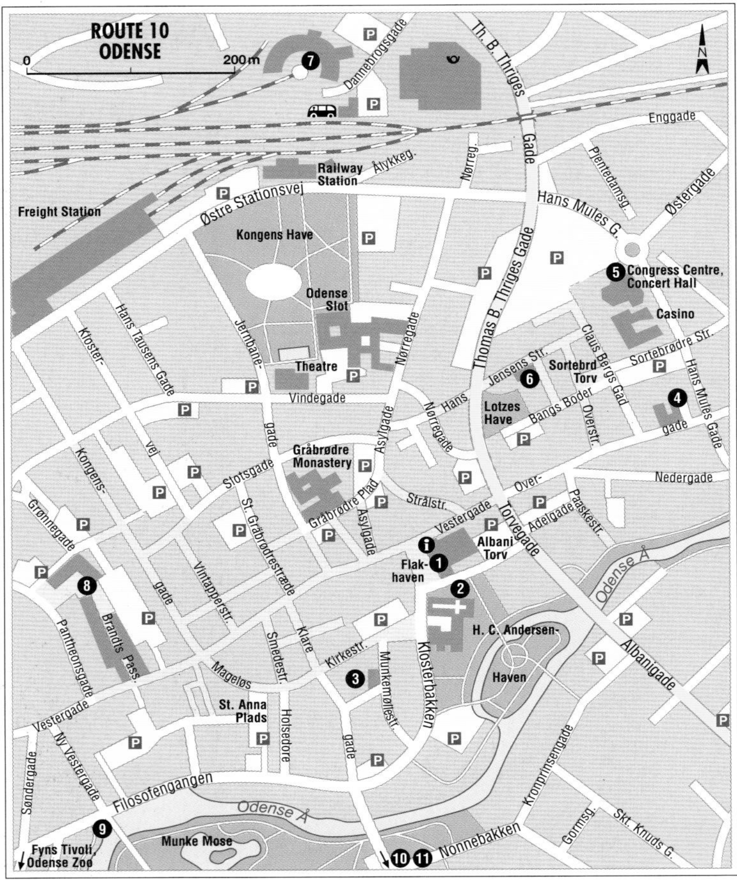

Odense, sacred in pagan times as the *vi*, or sanctuary of Odin, the Norse god of war, was first recorded in history in 988, when Emperor Otto III granted it certain tax privileges. At that time there was a Viking fort here similar to the one at Trelleborg (*see page 68*). King Knud (Canute) was murdered in the Sankt Albani Church in 1086 by rebellious subjects protesting against taxes levied to support raids against England. The pope responded by canonising the king, thus turning Odense into a place of pilgrimage. The construction of a harbour connected via a canal to the Baltic in 1804 brought about an economic upsurge. Today the city is profiting from the trend towards decentralisation in Denmark: for instance, it is the location of the country's second main television channel, TV2.

Odense Town Hall

Sights

The oldest section of **Odense Town Hall** ❶ (guided tours May to September) is the wing built in 1883, which is neoclassical in style with Gothic borrowings. To the south of it is the impressive Gothic ★ **St Knud's Cathedral** (*Sankt Knuds Kirke*) ❷. It contains a magnificent **golden altar** (1521) by Claus Berg, and the crypt holds royal tombs dating from the 16th century as well as the holy relics of St Knud. A monument between the present-day St Knud's Cathedral and the Town Hall marks the spot where the regicide took place.

Detail of the golden altar

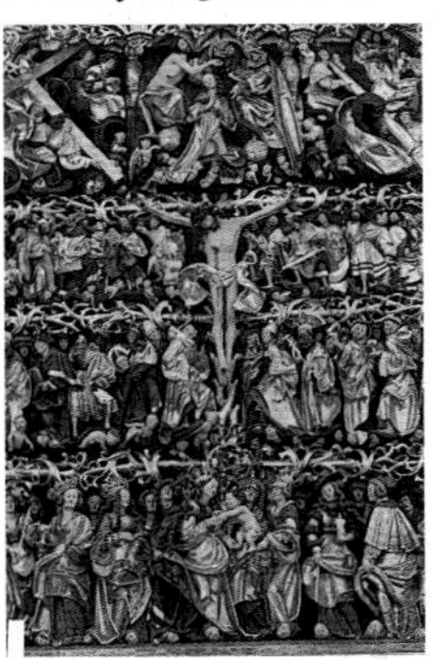

The street called **Munkemøllestræde** (Nos 3–5) contains the humble half-timbered **building** ❸ where Hans Christian Anderson spent his impoverished childhood. Beyond St Knud's Cathedral lies the idyllic **Hans Christian Andersen Park**, a good place to pause for a while. It contains a statue of the author, of course, alongside several other modern sculptures.

The Overgade is an attractive street, lined with charming half-timbered houses. Nos 48–50 contain the Museum of Civic History and also the so-called ★ **Møntergården** ❹, which has a very good coin collection.

From here it's only a few steps to the charmingly renovated 'poor quarter' of the town, bordered to the east by the modern congress centre with a concert hall, a **casino** and the ★ **Carl Nielsen Museum** ❺, (Claus Bergs Gade 11). The composer **Carl Nielsen** (1865–1931) is the second most famous native of Odense, after Hans Christian Andersen. At the centre of the district is ★★ **Hans Christian Andersen's Birthplace** ❻ (Hans Jensens Stræde 37–45). The little house with its large annexes has become a place of pilgrimage. Exhibits here include documents, letters, personal items, copies of Andersen's works in many different languages, and also the length of rope he always took with him whenever he travelled, to help him escape in case of fire.

Andersen's birthplace sign

Performer at the Andersen house

Westwards from the Town Hall the Vestergade is the most important shopping street in the city. One of the side-streets, Jernbanegade, leads north towards the station, and halfway along it is the ★ **Fyns Kunstmuseum** (Jernbanegade 13).

The route carries on now past **Odense Castle**, and through the park of **Kongens Have**, arriving at the railway

Art Museum, Brandt's Klaedefabrik

station; behind it, the ★ **Railway Museum** (*Jernbanemuseet*) ❼ (Dannebrogsgade 24; pedestrian access from station) is housed inside a former locomotive shed. The collection of royal carriages is especially impressive and should not be missed.

Further west along the Vestergade is the former textile factory known as ★★ **Brandt's Klædefabrik** ❽ (Brandts Passage 37–43), which has been the city's biggest attraction since the 1980s. It contains an ★ **Art Museum**, full of alternating exhibitions, a ★ **Museum of Photographic Art** and also a **Printing Museum** where various printing techniques are regularly demonstrated. A cinema, a café-restaurant, an open-air stage and pubs in the wings of the complex make the whole place into a cultural meeting-place *par excellence*. A little further south are the landing-stages of the **Odense Åfart** ❾ (Munke Moser/Filosofgangen). Taking the boat is the best way of reaching ★ **The Fyn Village** (*Den Fynske Landsby*) ❿ (Sejerskovvej 20) is an open-air museum comprising over 20 rural buildings from every part of Fyn, and craft exhibitions are held here in summer.

The Fyn Village

Still further south (around 8km/5 miles from the city centre, with good bus connections) is the **Hollufgård Museum Centre** ⓫ (Hestehaven 201), built on the site of a manor house dating from 1577. Exhibitions here document the history of the island of Fyn, and the spacious grounds of the museum contain reconstructions of dwellings from the Bronze and Viking Ages.

For more excursions in this area see Route 9, beginning on page 55.

Local fisherman

Route 11

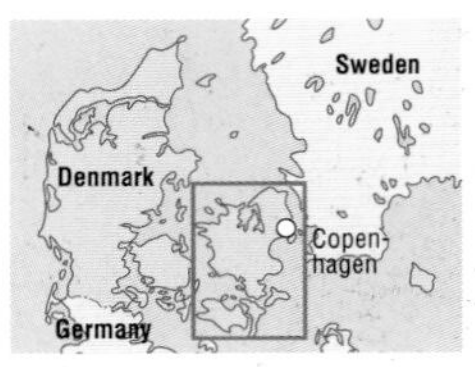

Route 11 comprises four journeys in Sjælland. The first two are journeys to Copenhagen from the important ferry harbours of Rødbyhavn, Korsør or Gedser. They use quiet, well-paved roads that run parallel to the motorways (switching between the two is possible at several locations). The third itinerary is a tour around Sjælland, and the fourth island-hops across the south.

Horse-drawn caravan

Route 11A – From the ferry ports in the south: Rødbyhavn/Gedser – Vordingborg – Copenhagen (150km/93 miles)

Route 11B – From the Great Belt Korsør – Sorø – Ringsted – Roskilde – Copenhagen (110km/68 miles)

Route 11C – Around Sjælland: Korsør – Næstved – Fakse – Copenhagen – Helsingør – Hundested – Nykøbing S. – Kalundborg – Korsør (300km/186 miles)

Route 11D – Island-Hopping: Møn – Stubbekøbing – Nykøbing F. – Nysted – Naksov – Tårs (158km/98 miles)

Route 11A

Rødbyhavn, or just Rødby for short, has been the Danish ferry port with the most direct access to the south since 1963. From here the road leads inland to **Maribo** (pop. 5,500, 18km/11 miles), which lies in an area full of lakes. There are exhibitions of Danish art of various epochs at the Maribo Museum on the square. An ★ open-air folklore museum is also worth a visit. The cathedral church (1470) on the banks of the Søndersø was originally part of a convent. On the right of the choir is the grave of Leonara Christina (1621–98), who died in Maribo. Though the favourite daughter of King Christian IV, she married a plotting husband and spent 22 years in prison. Her life story, *Jammers Minde*, is a classic of Danish literature.

Maribo Cathedral

During the summer a vintage railway connects Maribo with Bandholm on the north coast of Lolland. Several exotic species of animal can be admired here at the ★ **Knuthenborg Safari Park.**

Take a ride on the vintage railway

Road number 153 crosses the Guldborg Sund and, shortly afterwards, the the straits of Storstrømmen. The 3,200-m (10,500-ft) long Storstrømsbro for road and rail traffic was considered a major engineering feat in its time. A more modern bridge is the Farø Bridge (1985, total length 3,322m/10,900ft), which was built to accommodate the E47/55 motorway.

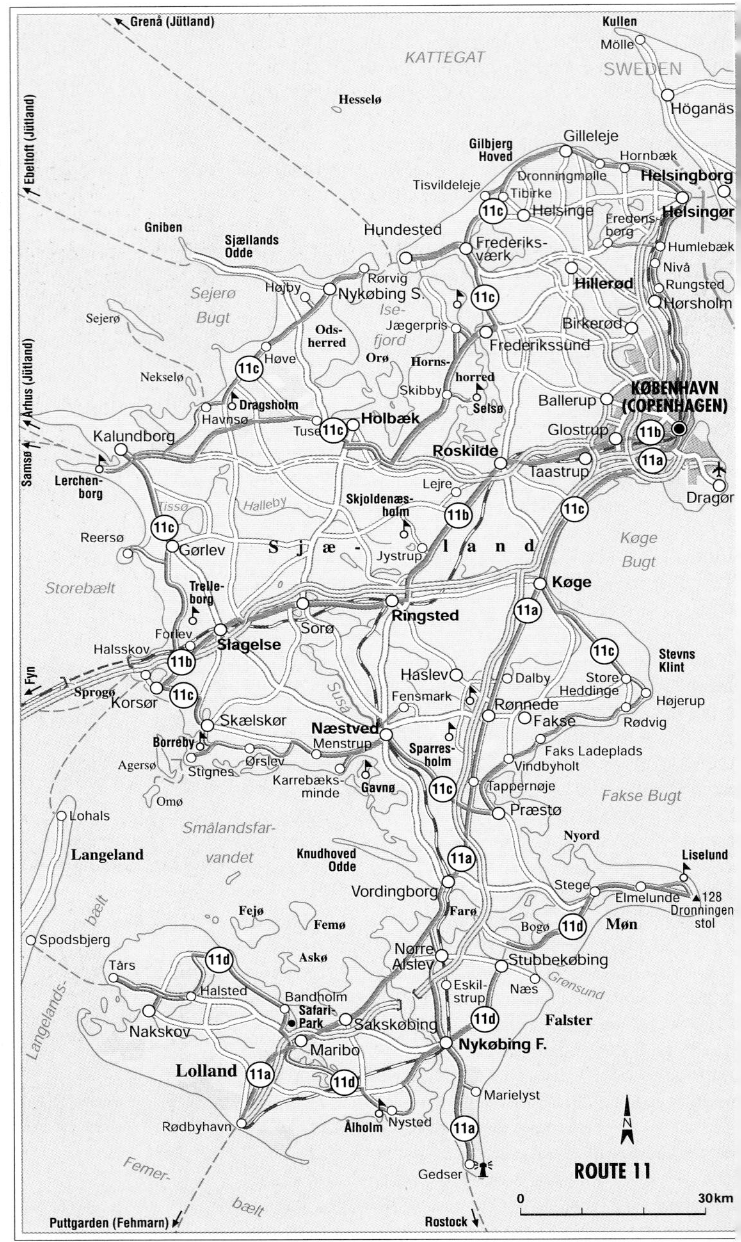
Grenå (Jütland)
KATTEGAT
Kullen
Mölle
SWEDEN
Höganäs
Hesselø
Ebeltoft (Jütland)
Gilbjerg Hoved
Gilleleje
Hornbæk
Dronningmølle
Helsingborg
Tisvildeleje
Tibirke
Helsinge
Helsingør
Gniben
Sjællands Odde
Hundested
Frederiksværk
Fredensborg
Humlebæk
Nivå
Rørvig
Hillerød
Rungsted
Sejerø Bugt
Højby
Nykøbing S.
Hørsholm
Sejerø
Isefjord
Jægerpris
Birkerød
Odsherred
Frederikssund
Århus (Jütland)
Høve
Orø
Hornsherred
Nekselø
Skibby
Selsø
Ballerup
KØBENHAVN (COPENHAGEN)
Dragsholm
Havnsø
Holbæk
Tuse
Glostrup
Kalundborg
Roskilde
Samsø
Lerchenborg
Taastrup
Dragør
Lejre
Tissø
Halleby
Skjoldenæsholm
Reersø
Gørlev
Sjælland
Jystrup
Køge Bugt
Storebælt
Trelleborg
Køge
Sorø
Ringsted
Forlev
Halsskov
Slagelse
Stevns Klint
Fyn
Haslev
Dalby
Store Heddinge
Sprogø
Korsør
Fensmark
Højerup
Rønnede
Fakse
Rødvig
Skælskør
Næstved
Susă
Borreby
Menstrup
Faks Ladeplads
Agersø
Sparresholm
Vindbyholt
Ørslev
Stignes
Karrebæksminde
Gavnø
Tappernøje
Omø
Fakse Bugt
Præstø
Lohals
Smålandsfarvandet
Nyord
Langeland
Knudhoved Odde
Liselund
Vordingborg
Stege
Elmelunde
128
Dronningen stol
Langelandsbælt
Fejø
Farø
Bogø
Møn
Femø
Spodsbjerg
Askø
Nørre Alslev
Stubbekøbing
Tårs
Grønsund
Halsted
Eskilstrup
Næs
Bandholm
Safari-Park
Sakskøbing
Falster
Nakskov
Maribo
Nykøbing F.
Lolland
Marielyst
Rødbyhavn
Ålholm
Nysted
Femerbælt
Gedser
ROUTE 11
0
30 km
Puttgarden (Fehmarn)
Rostock
11a
11b
11c
11d
N

Gedser (pop. 1,000) has been a ferry harbour since 1903, with connections to Rostock. The southernmost part of Denmark, Gedser Odde, is marked by the massive square lighthouse of Gedser Fyr, which can be ascended.

To the north a broad, 20-km (12-mile) long ★ sandy beach extends along the east coast of Falstewr. **Nykøbing F.** (pop. 19,000, 24km/15 miles), the capital of Falster, is famous for its sugar factories. Among the half-timbered houses in the town centre is Czarens Hus, so named because Tsar Peter the Great dined in the restaurant which was here in 1717. There is a regional museum in the same building. On the opposite shore of the sound is the open-air ★★ **Middelaldercenter**, where medieval crafts are practised. The highlight of the centre is a demonstration of a huge reconstructed catapult in action.

Making coins, Middelaldercenter

Passing Eskilstrup and crossing the E47/E55, the Gedser variant meets up with Route 11A again at the Storstrømsbro on the road from Brødby.

Vordingborg (pop. 8600, 53km/32 miles), was used by Valdemar the Great (1154–82) as a base for raids against the Wends, and Valdemar Atterdag (1340–75) had a fortress built here in the mid-14th century to keep the Hanse at bay. Parts of the fortress wall and its 26-m (85-ft) high ★ Goose Tower (*Gåsetårn*) have been preserved to this day. Near the tower is a local museum and also a historical-botanical herb garden.

The local museum, Vordingborg

The narrow promontory of **Knudhoved Odde** nearby has prehistoric sites as well as a bison park.

Near **Tappernøje** (71km/44 miles), it is possible to switch to Route 12 (*see page 76*). Soon afterwards you can take a worthwhile detour to three manor houses: **Sparresholm** (17th-century), southwest of Rønnede (82km/51 miles); the Renaissance manor of **Gisselfeld** (mid-16th-century) further north, which has one of the finest parks in Denmark; and near Dalby (88km/55 miles), **Bregentved Manor** can be visited. The latter was built in the late 19th century, but in 18th-century rococo style, based on plans by N Eigtved, the architect of Amalienborg.

Gisselfeld Manor

Køge (pop. 31,500, 107km/66 miles), is an old harbour town whose market square is flanked by charming half-timbered buildings (1527 onwards). The ★ Køge Sketch Museum records the construction of some of them. Also well worth a visit is the ★ Sankt Nicolai Kirke, which has one of Denmark's most beautiful town church interiors.

The route then carries on along Køge Bay, where a recreation park has been established among the dunes and lagoons. At the centre of this seascape, near the Ishøj marina, is a new museum of contemporary art, whose unusual ship-like shape has led it to be called simply ★★ **Arken** (The Ark). From here the centre of **Copenhagen** (*see page 18*), 150km (93 miles), is visible on the horizon.

Route 11B

Korsør (pop. 14,800) is Sjælland's traditional bridgehead to Fyn (*see Route 9*) In earlier days the winds weren't always right for the crossing, and the best place to wait for them to change was in the King's Courtyard (*Kongsgården*) in the Algasde, where royalty sometimes dined; the sandstone statues next to the front door depict the four seasons. A fortress tower (partly 13th-century) and a complex of out buildings (today housing the Civic Museum) are all that remain of a medieval fortress that once stood at the harbour entrance.

King's Courtyard, detail

Next to the car ferry docks at Halsskov is another information office about construction work on the Record Bridge (*see page 57*).

Route 11B now turns eastwards. To the north of Forlev (10km/6 miles) is the Viking fort of ★★ **Trelleborg**, which dates from 980 (ie the reign of Harald Bluetooth, *see page 11*, 950). There were four of these forts in Denmark, but only Fyrkat near Hobro (*see page 39*) is in a similarly good state of preservation. The Viking house at the entrance to the fort has been faithfully reconstructed. On a cold day it is easy to understand how tough life must have been, hardy though the Vikings were.

A Trelleborg Viking

★ **Sorø** (pop. 6,300, 31km/19 miles), grew up around a monastery built by the Cistercians in 1161 under the protection of Bishop Absalon (1154–82, *see page 11*). Survivors of this former structure are the gatehouse and the ★ church (concert series, *see page 81*); both are among the most important medieval buildings in Denmark. There are two interesting ★ crucifixes inside the church: one by Claus Berg (8m/26ft high, in the central nave) and a late 13th-century one in the northern transept. Absalon, several kings and the poet Ludvig Holberg (1648–1754) are all buried here.

The monastery was turned into a boarding school in 1586, and became a riding academy in 1623. The neoclassical main building on the banks of the lake is very imposing; it was officially opened in 1826.

The West Sjælland Museum of Art contains an important collection of art dating from the so-called Golden Age (*see page 12*) as well as medieval ecclesiastical art and several modern canvases.

Ringsted (pop. 17,000, 46km/28 miles), was one of the country's major towns in the Middle Ages and was the centre of Sjælland's *things* (arbitrating assemblies). The ★ **Skt Bendts Kirke** is part of a former Benedictine monastery, and was erected on the site of a former structure. It is dedicated to all Danish kings who bear the name of Valdemar, and inside, 27 kings lie buried. There are also some fine frescoes on spiritual and secular themes dating from the 13th to 19th century.

St Bendts Church ceiling

Route 11B now changes over to road number 14. Near **Jystrup**, 56km (35 miles), there is a good tram museum and also the highest peak in Sjælland, the 126-m (410-ft) high Gyldenløveshøj.

A few kilometres to the west of the village of Lejre (69km/43 miles) is the archaeological centre of ★★ **Lejre Oldtidsbyen**. Scientific theories about earlier epochs are being put to the test here in a series of practical experiments. Not far away is a building from quite another era: the ornate rococo castle of ★ **Ledreborg**.

Statue at Ledreborg

★★ **Roskilde** (pop. 40,000, 76km/47 miles) had the chance of becoming Denmark's capital but was finally superseded by Copenhagen on account of the latter's superior access for shipping. ★★ **Roskilde Cathedral** is the third or fourth structure on the site. The present-day edifice dates back to Bishop Absalon (*see page 11*) but was only completed in the late 13th century (Romanesque-Gothic). Ten later extensions have added architectural variety. It is the burial place of generations of Danish monarchs and a total of 38 kings and queens are entombed here, from Magrethe I (died 1412) right up to Frederick IX (died 1972). An ancient bridge connects the choir with the episcopal palace, where a modern art exhibition can be admired.

Roskilde Cathedral, detail

The ★★ **Viking Ship Hall** situated on the banks of the Roskilde Fjord contains five Viking ships of different types that are thought to have sunk roughly 20km (12 miles) up the fjord around AD1000. The vessels were recovered in 1962 and have been restored as far as possible. A view of the fjord can be had through a large window beyond the ships.

Viking Ship Hall

It's only a short trip from Roskilde to Copenhagen (*see page 18*) (110km/68 miles). There's a wide choice of different directions along the motorway ring road.

Route 11C

This tour of Sjælland begins (like Route 11B) in the harbour town of Korsør (*see page 68*), from where it proceeds in a southerly direction.

Tram in Skaelskor

Skælskør (pop. 6,000, 12km/7½ miles), is a pleasant harbour town. The lagoons and swampy areas around here are a paradise for ornithologists, despite the nearby oil refinery. From **Stignes** one can reach the attractive islands and day-trip destinations of ★ **Agersø** (pop. 250, 684ha/1,698 acres) and **Omø** (pop. 170, 452ha/1,116 acres).

Route 11C only uses side roads now, but they're all part of the well-signposted Daisy Route. The tall and imposing-looking Renaissance manor of ★ **Borreby** (15km/9 miles) has a courtyard and a park open to the public. The pilgrimage church of ★ **Ørslev** (24km/15 miles) dates from the early Middle Ages and is famous for its frescoe, as well as the fact that the counts of Holsteinborg are buried there.

Holsteinborg Manor

The four-winged Renaissance manor of ★ **Holsteinborg** (26km/16 miles) was one of the favourite retreats of the author Hans Christian Andersen.

Passing through **Menstrup** (37km/23 miles) and the famous bathing resort of **Karrebæksminde**, the route arrives at ★ **Næstved** (pop. 38,500, 49km/30 miles), the garrison town of the royal hussars. The part of town around Axeltorv contains some of the oldest stone houses in Denmark (15th- and 16th-century). The two medieval churches Sankt Peters Kirke and Sankt Mortens Kirke contain fine frescoes; the latter also boasts a late baroque altar screen by Abel Schrøder the Younger and a chancel by his father.

To the north of the town, the highly regarded boarding school of Herlufsholm (founded in 1560 by Admiral Herluf Trolle) is housed inside a former monastery. The old monastery church, which dates from around 1200, has an unusual crucifix made of walrus ivory.

At the glassworks

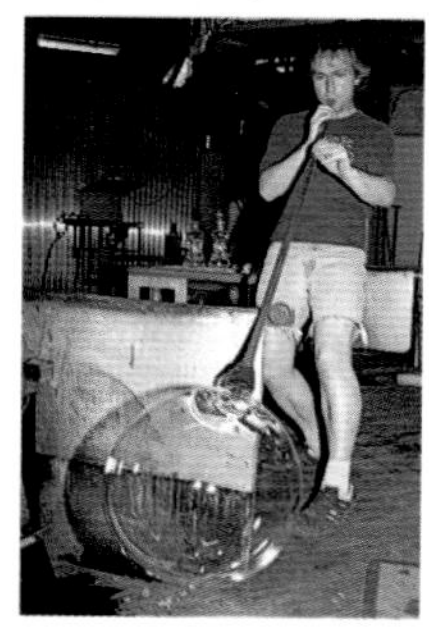

The world-famous **Holmegaard glassworks** are situated to the northwest of Næstved in **Fensmark** (museum, plus cheap sales from factory). To the south of the town is the attractive castle of ★ **Gavnø** with its impressive collection of paintings, a fire-engine exhibition and a butterfly house. The upper reaches of the Suså river, which runs through Næstved, are a popular canoeing area.

On the east coast of Sjælland is the little town of **Præstø** (73km/45 miles), which has a fire brigade museum. North of the town is the Bysø mansion (1673), which was a centre of intellectual and artistic life during the so-called Golden Age (*see page 12*). Bertel Thorvaldsen (*see page 80*) had a studio here; today it is a miniature museum containing several of his works.

Route 11C now continues northwards and turns off on to side roads at Vindbyholt in the direction of **Fakse**

Ladeplads (pop. 2,500, 93km/58 miles), a harbour town with popular beaches. At the harbour in **Rødvig** (111km/69 miles), look out for an unusual-looking kiln; this was originally used for firing powdered flint to make the glaze for porcelain.

Chalk cliffs of Stevns Klint

The chalk cliffs known as ★ **Stevns Klint** begin to the east of Rødvig. The old ★★ church at **Højerup** looks very dramatic: in 1928 its choir section fell into the sea; the rest is on the brink of following suit.

At **Store Hedding** (119km/74 miles), there is an originally ★ Romanesque church of a design unique in Denmark: the nave is octagonal, and there is a fine pillared gallery on the second storey of the choir.

Store Hedding church

From Køge (140km/87 miles) (*see page 67*) it is possible either to to take the 151 into Copenhagen (180km/112 miles) or to drive around the capital along the circular E47/55. The route then continues northwards along the coast road, with a mixture of old and new beach resorts, and pretty scenery.

Near Klampenborg (190km/118 miles) the ★★ Ordrupgaardsamlingen in **Ordrup** contains a number of fine French paintings, including works by Gauguin, Monet, Degas and other French impressionists. Finds from the 7,000-year-old ★ **Vedbæk grave** (200km/124 miles) are on display at the nearby ★ **Gammel Holtegård**. In **Hørsholm** there is an important ★ hunting and forestry museum, containing weapons and trophies dating from the Ice Age to the present.

Manet painting in Ordrup gallery

The country house of Rungstedlund in the neighbouring coastal town of Rungsted (205km/127 miles) contains the ★ **Karen Blixen Museum**. The famous authoress of *Out of Africa* (1885–1962) lived here for many years, and is buried in a simple grave under a beech tree behind the house. The small museum on the Nivågård estate in **Nivå** (210km/130 miles) has a collection of Italian and Dutch Renaissance art.

Karen Blixen

★★★ **Louisiana**, the museum for modern art in **Humlebæk** (215km/133 miles) is one of the most important museums in Europe. The bulk of the permanent collection comprises works by Danish and international artists since World War II; there are also regular temporary exhibitions. The museum buildings situated in an old park above the Sound are an experience in themselves, and the lawns here are dotted with sculptures by Max Ernst, Calder and Henry Moore.

★★ **Fredensborg Palace**, a fine baroque building just 10km (6 miles) inland, is the home of the Danish royal family during early and late summer; at these times of the year public access to the palace is limited, but it is still worth coming to see the grandiose changing of the guard ceremony.

Sankt Mariae Kirke

Helsingør (pop. 44,000, 225km/140 miles), also called Elsinore, has a fine old town section with many attractive houses. The street known as Gl. Færgestræde in particular has retained a strong medieval flavour, without any modern shops. The most important building in the town centre is the well-preserved early 16th-century Carmelite monastery with its ★ Sankt Mariæ Kirke. The famous composer Buxtehude was the organist here from 1660–8, and the organ (1635) he played can still be admired. The history section of the Civic Museum is in the monastery's former almshouses.

Chapel of Kronborg Slot

The main sight at Helsingør, though, is ★★ **Kronborg Slot**, the Renaissance castle that guards the harbour entrance. Its chapel and ★★ banquet hall are especially notable; it also contains a ★ trade and seafaring museum. The castle played a major role in collecting tolls for crossing the Sound (1425–1857, *see pages 11* and *12*), but is most famous as the Elsinore Castle of Shakespeare's *Hamlet*.

The ★ **Denmark Technical Museum** has two departments on the outskirts of Helsingør, one in the southwest and the other, main one to the northeast where the coast road (Route 11C) leaves the town. The neoclassical **Marienlyst Castle** (Civic Museum art collection) is also situated here.

Rudolf Tegner Museum

The first real coastal resort to the west of Helsingør is ★ **Hornbæk** (237km/147 miles), with a large marina. Just 2km (1 mile) inland from Dronningmølle (241km/149 miles), on a bleak stretch of moor, is the Rudolf Tegner Museum (1938), which resembles a bunker on the outside and a studio on the inside; there are several large sculptures by this controversial artist (1873–1950) displayed in a park close by.

★ **Gilleleje** (pop. 4,700, 250km/155 miles) is the hub of tourism on the Sjælland coast and it has several

Lazy afternoon in a Gilleleje café

attractions – including deep-sea fishing. A path west of the town leads to the steep coast of Gilbjerg Hoved, over 300m (980ft) high in places and marking the border between the Kattegat and the Sound; there are several fine views from here. This was also a favourite haunt of the philosopher Søren Kierkegaard (*see page 80*), commemorated by a memorial plaque.

The Gilleleje Museum concentrates on fishing and seafaring; and the Villa Munkeruphus, to the east of the town, holds arts and crafts exhibitions.

Tisvildeleje (265km/165 miles) is another attractive beach resort. It is bordered to the west by one of the finest forests in northern Sjælland, **Tisvilde Hegn**. The isolated Tibirke Kirke, 4km (2½ miles) inland (ornate Gothic altar), is all that remains of a village which was destroyed by sand drift.

Knud Rasmussen Hus

Hundested (pop. 8,000, 290km/180 miles) is situated above the Kattegat and contains the **Knud Rasmussen Hus**, a museum in memory of the Arctic explorer.

Route 11C now takes the ferry (hourly, 25 minutes travel time) across the mouth of the Ise Fjord. An alternative route here is to turn inland in the direction of Frederikssund (Viking games, *see page 81*;★ J F Willumsen Museum) and cross the Hornsherred peninsula (Jægerspris Castle and ★★ Selsø Castle near Skibby). Two of the churches here, near Holbæk, are famed for their frescoes: ★ Tuse (Gothic) and ★ Tveje Merløse (Romanesque).

Tuse Church is famed for its frescoes

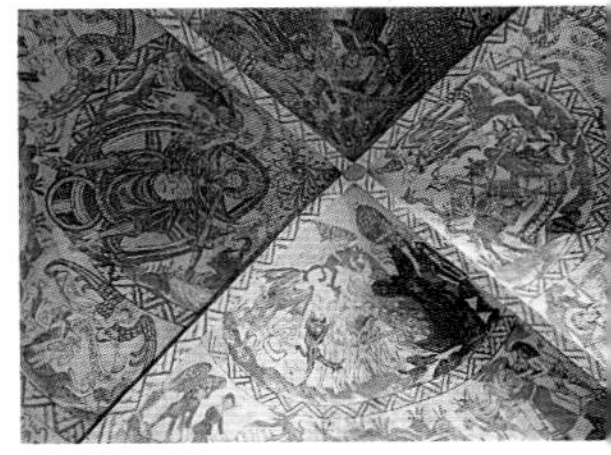

Those who take the ferry will end up in Rørvig on the ★★ **Odsherred peninsula**, a region steeped in history, with many fine medieval churches, prehistoric sites and fine local museums as well as plenty of holiday homes and fine, safe beaches. At the end of the narrow promontory of Sjællands Odde is a ferry harbour with regular connections to Ebeltoft in Jutland (*see page 54*), and on Gniben Point there are several plaques in honour of individuals who have swum from here to Jutland.

★ **Nykøbing Sjælland** (pop. 5,000, 297km/184 miles) is the main town of Odsherred. The Annebjerg Collection has some fine specimens of glassware dating from antiquity to the present day.

In **Højby**, a few kilometres to the west, is the imposing Romanesque ★ Højby Kirke, which has many fine frescoes. There is also a good amusement park, Sommerland Sjælland, to the south of the town. In 1902, on the moor of Trundholm, almost on the west coast, the Bronze Age ★★ **Trundholm Sun-Chariot** (*Trundholm Solvogn*) was discovered: a golden solar disc on six narrow wheels, drawn by a horse. The original is in the Copenhagen National Museum, and there is a copy in the local museum at Høve. The chariot represents the earliest-known use of spokes for wheels in Denmark.

Højby Kirke altar

Route 11C now follows the Daisy Route along side-roads through some beautiful coastal scenery via Havnsø as far as road number 23.

Kalundborg (pop. 15,500, 250km/155 miles) is an important industrial town (power station, refinery). At its centre is the 12th-century ★★ **Church of Our Lady** (*Vor Frue Kirke*), the ground-plan of which is in the form of a Greek cross – something quite unique in Danish church architecture. The middle tower collapsed in 1827 but has been faithfully restored. The late medieval houses around the church are most attractive.

Church of Our Lady, Kalundborg

Lerchenborg Manor, with its magnificent baroque gardens, is just a few kilometres to the south of Kalundborg; its grand banqueting hall is open to the public during the summer months.

The route travels southwards now via **Gørlev** (270km/168 miles). A possible detour could be made at this point to the picturesque village of **Reersø**, where time does seem to have stood still. Passing close to Trelleborg (*see page 68*), the route then reaches its starting-point again at Korsør (*see page 68*), (300km (186 miles).

Route 11D

This 'island-hopping' route across Møn, Falster and Lolland begins at the 128-m (420-ft) high ★★ **Queen's Chair** (*Dronningenstol*), the highest 'peak' of the ★★ **chalk cliffs of Møn**. This impressive steep coast extends a distance of roughly 12km (7½ miles), from the Møns Fyr lighthouse in the south to the 27-m (88-ft) high Brunhoved in the north. The chalk cliffs are nearly 75 million years old, and packed with fossils.

Møn's chalk cliffs

Above the northern part of the cliffs, the thatched roof of the miniature castle of ★ **Liselund** (1792) can be seen; it has a romantic garden.

Møn not only has fantastic scenery to offer visitors; it also has several important ★ prehistoric sites. There are also many churches famed for their frescoes, including some of the best Europe has to offer – in particular those by the so-called Elmelunde Master in the ★★ **Elmelunde Kirke** (11km/6 miles), the ★ **Kelby Kirke** (15km/9 miles), and the ★★ **Fanefjord Kirke** (West-Møn, 30km/18 miles). In **Stege** (19km/12 miles), Møn's largest town, there is a 16th-century town gate, and next door to it an interesting local museum.

Elmelunde Kirke

Route 11D leads across western Møn and then across an embankment (1943) to the island of **Bogø** (37km/22 miles). Marvellously nostalgic old ferry boats cross the Grønsund here, but going via the island of Farø and the motorway is the quickest route to **Stubbekøbing** (pop. 2,300) on **Falster**. A Motorcycle and Radio Museum here contains over 250 ancient bikes and a hi-fi exhibition;

Vintage cars in Nysted

the inventor of the dynamic loudspeaker is a native of the town.

Route 11D leads via Nykøbing F (58km/36 miles); *see also* Route 11A, *page 65*) to Lolland and then on to **Nysted** (pop. 1,500, 78km/48 miles). This pretty little harbour town is overlooked by ★ **Alholm Slot**, considered by many to be the oldest inhabited castle in the world (sections dating from around 1300); there are several exhibitions inside catering to a broad range of tastes. A mini-railway chugs through the castle estate, and there is also a hall containing around 250 vintage cars – one of the best collections of pre-World War II cars in all Europe.

Alholm Slot: the lounge

To the west of Nysted, near Stubberup, two scientists are carrying out a series of behavioural experiments on wolves at the Engholm Wolfscenter.

Route 11D now follows the Daisy Route through the lake area and to Maribo (107km/66 miles; Route 11B, *see page 68*), and then on across the northern part of Lolland. The point where the Daisy Route branches off the 289 is the start of a *mil* (an old mile, roughly 7.5km/4 miles) marked out by ancient milestones. On the edges of the *mil* are Kong Svends Høj (133km/82 miles), a burial chamber 12.5m (41ft) in length, and Pederstrup mansion with a memorial museum to the agricultural reformer CD Reventlow (*see page 12*).

Near the former Benedictine monastery of Haldsted (144km/89 miles), the route joins road No 9, which leads to the ferry docks at Tårs (158km/98 miles). From here you should take the ferry to Spodsbjerg on Langeland (travelling time is approximately 45 minutes; *see also* Route 9B, *page 59*).

Naksov (150km/93 miles, pop. 15,000), is an old shipbuilding town currently suffering from recession. There are excursions on the post boat across to the little islands in Naksov Fjord.

Naksov fisherman

Stavns Fjord

Samsø and Bornholm

Islands well worth a visit

★★ *Samsø*

This island of Samsø (pop. 4,300) lies between Jutland, Fyn and Sjælland. It measures just 28km (17 miles) by 7km (4 miles). Nevertheless, the island is often seen as having two parts, for the northern and southern parts of Samsø are separated by a very narrow strip of land, and rumour has it that the inhabitants of the two halves don't get on that well. The main source of income is agriculture. Samsø potatoes – the earliest crop north of the Alps – are well-known.

The history of Samsø is as old as that of Denmark itself, as evidenced by numerous ★ prehistoric sites. These cannot be missed in the south of the island: almost every mound has a Stone Age or Bronze Age grave on top of it. The ★★ **Stavns Fjord** was an important assembly area for ships during the Viking Age. Archaeologists have discovered a quay dating from early Viking times and the route of the 800-m (2,620-ft) long and 11-m (36-ft) wide ★ **Kanhave Canal** running from the east to the west coast; the tree trunks used to reinforce the canal banks were felled in 726.

A Nordby house

★ **Nordby**, the 'metropolis' of northern Samsø, is one of the prettiest villages in Denmark. The church, once the parish church for three villages, is around 1.5km (1 mile) outside the village. The belltower in the village itself was built in 1857. The island's capital of **Tranebjerg** has a fine ★ church.

Samsø also has some splendid natural scenery, including ★ **Nordby Bakker** (hiking paths, view across to Jutland and Sjælland coasts from 64-m/210-ft high Ballbjerg) and the set of islands in ★★ Stavns Fjord.

★★★ Bornholm

The island of Bornholm (pop. 45,000) is popular as a travel destination in its own right, but thanks to Denmark's efficient ferry connections it can also easily form part of a round trip through the country. Once on the island, nothing's very far away from anything else (max 44km/27 miles, or 1 hour's drive).

Bornholm is Denmark's only rocky island, and is more reminiscent of Norway than of Jutland. ★★ **Hammeren**, the barren granite region in the north, is a conservation area. Southern Bornholm, with its flat coast, is similar to the rest of Denmark, the highlight being the ★★ sandy beach of Dueodde.

Bornholm's distinguishing features are its four ★★ **round churches** dating from the early days of the Danes' conversion to Christianity. The largest one is the ★★ **Østerlarskirke** near Gudhjem. Seven external buttresses give it stability, and inside, the mighty middle pillar, decorated with complex frescoes depicting the life of Christ, has enough room inside it for a baptismal chapel. In the north of Bornholm the rather isolated ★★ **Olskirke** also serves as a landmark for sailors. The ★ **Nylarskirke**, east of Rønne, is distinctive for its lack of external supporting pillars, while the ★ **Nykirke**, to the north of Rønne, is one storey smaller than the other three.

The origin of the round churches is obscure, but they were probably built as fortress-churches in the 12th and 13th centuries. Their pointed roofs were added later.

High on a rock above the island's rocky north coast is the picturesque ruined castle of ★★ **Hammershus**, the former stronghold of the bishops of Lund.

The island's towns all have idyllic corners with tiny winding streets and lots of colourful half-timbered houses. ★★ **Svaneke** on the east coast is particularly harmonious. Various craftsmen (including ★ glassblowers) have set up workshops near the marketplace. Another must is a stroll through the cobbled streets in the old section of ★ **Rønne**.

Bornholm has over a dozen **museums**. A real highlight at the ★★ **Bornholms Museum** in Rønne are the ★★ ***Goldgubber***, small beaten plates of gold, which were probably offertories from the Germanic Iron Age (c 6th-century). These treasures were found near Svaneke during the 1980s. Directly above the spectacular steep coast of ★ **Helligdommen**, near Rønne, is the ★★ **Bornholm Museum of Art** (for more details on the Bornholm and other groups of painters, *see page 80*).

The ★★ **Ertholmene** skerry group (40ha/98 acres, pop. 120), lying almost 20km (12½ miles) off the north coast, is popular among day-trippers. This group of islands is a conservation area, and a small community of fishermen and artists lives here all year round.

Taking it easy on Bornholm

Hammeren granite massif

Østerlarskirke round church

The Goldgrubber

Art History

Architecture

There are megalithic tombs dating from the Stone Age (3500–1800BC) to be found in most parts of Denmark: round dolmens, or *runddysse* (individual burial chambers) are the oldest variety. These were followed by long dolmens, or *langdysse* (one or more burial chambers in a rectangular area), and then by chamber tombs used for several interments, known in Danish as *jættestue* (accessible via a passageway from the side).

Ship monuments (graves enclosed by standing stones in the form of a ship) were common during the Late Iron Age and Viking Age (ca AD800–1035). The ramparts of the Viking forts at Trelleborg *(see page 68)* and at Fyrkat *(see page 39)* are laid out with remarkable precision.

During the Romanesque period (1035–1250) many cathedrals were built (including Ribe, *see page 29*, and Viborg, *see page 54*) and more than 1,000 rural churches made of granite. Many of today's village churches have Romanesque cores, but were later adapted to suite other styles. It was also during this period that the first castles (eg Nyborg, *see page 56*) were built. The cathedral of Roskilde *(see page 69)* demonstrates the transition from Romanesque to the Gothic style (1250–1550). New churches in the countryside were now mostly built of brick.

The Renaissance (1550–1630) was strongly Dutch in flavour, and left Denmark with a magnificent series of structures including Kronborg Castle *(see page 72)*, and the buildings erected during the reign of Christian IV. Many of the country's most famous manor houses also date from this period (including Egeskov, *page 56*; Voergård, *page 37*); other interesting buildings include Jens Bangs Stenhus (Ålborg, *page 34*) and several other magnificent half-timbered houses in the provincial towns.

The baroque style (1630–1735) also arrived in Denmark via Holland: good examples here are Charlottenborg Palace *(see page 22)*, Fredensborg *(see page 71)* as well as the Church of Our Saviour in Copenhagen. The finest examples of the style that followed, rococo (1735–75), are Amalienborg Palace *(see page 23)*, today the royal residence, and the Prinsens Palæ, today the National Museum *(see page 20)*, both of them designed by Niels N Eigtved.

CF Hansen (1775–1850) was the Classical architect who redesigned much of Copenhagen after the fire of 1807; two of his works are Copenhagen Cathedral, and the Law Courts on the Nytorv. The architecture of the neoclassical era (1850–1930) borrows heavily from historical precedents, typical examples being the town halls of Odense (1880-83) and of Copenhagen (1895–1902). The town hall of Århus (1938–42) displays the quantum leap

Opposite: the ceiling fresco in Elmelunde Church

Ship grave from the Viking age

The nave of Ribe Cathedral

Kronborg Castle

Half-timbered house in Nyborg

Bornholm Art Museum

to functionalism, a style which is still in evidence today, especially in the area of design. Arne Jakobsen, who also helped to build the town hall in Århus, went on to become one of Europe's most famous architects.

Jørn Utzon's design for the Sydney Opera House proves that Danish architects are still very much in international demand. His other works include a water-tower in Svaneke (Bornholm) and the Paustean House in Copenhagen's northern harbour; he also did the plans for the modernisation of the *Langeliniekajs* in Copenhagen. Many of Denmark's museums of modern art are also highlights of contemporary architecture: the Trapholt Art Museum in Kolding (see *page 40*); the Louisiana (see *page 71*) and the Bornholm Museum of Art (*see page* 77).

Craftsmanship and the Fine Arts

Trundholm Sun-Chariot

Lurs (trumpets shaped like mammoth tusks), bronze wind instruments and the Bronze Age Trundholm Sun Chariot testify to the high level of craftsmanship during prehistoric times, as do the silver cauldron of Gundestrup and the golden horns of Gallehus.

In Romanesque times the churches were painted with frescoes that were later frequently Gothicised. Fresco painting reached its heyday in around 1500 (eg The Elmelunde Master of Møn). Two masterly exponents of wood-carving during the Gothic period were Bern Notke (altar of Århus Cathedral) and Claus Berg (altar of St Knud's Cathedral in Odense).

Ceiling fresco in Hojby Church

The first half of the 19th century, however, was the Golden Age of artistic and intellectual life in Denmark, especially in painting, as represented by CW Eckersberg, C Købke and JT Lundbye. Bertel Thorvaldsen, a neo-classical sculptor, achieved fame far beyond his country's borders. Other contemporaries included the author Hans Christian Andersen and philosopher Søren Kierkegaard.

The beginning of the 20th century saw fresh artistic impulses. Skagen *(see page 33)* was the workplace of two Impressionist painters, A Ancher and PS Krøyer. The Skagen painters were followed by the Fyn ones (Johannes Larsen, Anna and Fritz Syberg) and later Bornholm painters such as Oluf Høst.

Hans Christian Andersen

The CoBrA artists also achieved international importance after the war, especially Asger Jorn (collection in Silkeborg art museum) and Carl-Henning Petersen (museum in Henning). Until his death in 1993, Robert Jacobsen (monumental metal sculptures in the Tørskind gravel-pits near Egtved) was among the most prolific artists in the country. Also internationally famous is the painter, sculptor, film director and songwriter Per Kirkeby. Bjørn Nørgaard achieved national recognition with his massive building-art project.

The reconstructed Viking house at Trelleborg

Festivals and Folklore

Major open-air events dominate the cultural calendar in summer. These big festivals, which last several days and are famous far beyond Denmark's borders, include the one at Roskilde (end of June/beginning of July, with rock and pop), and at Tønder (August, with jazz, folk and soul). Well-known rock festivals include the one at Skanderborg held over the second weekend in August, and the Langeland Rock Festival in July.

In July there is a huge jazz festival in Copenhagen lasting several days. Århus has a festival week at the beginning of September with a wide range of cultural events (theatre, concerts, ballet, etc).

Classical music series are also very popular, especially those held in the church of Sorø and the cathedral in Ribe. Odense has an organ festival and, of course, there are the big events in Copenhagen's Tivoli Gardens as well as ballet festivals centred around the world famous Royal Danish Ballet. Classical concerts performed in the serene environment of some of the country's finest stately homes and palaces can be a very rewarding experience.

Jazz musicians

One of the most colourful epochs in Northern Europe's history, the Viking era, is brought vividly back to life in the Viking festivals. The most traditional of these is the one at Frederikssund (Sjælland) in the second half of June; there is a magnificent one on the open-air stage at Jells Lake in southern Jutland; and a Viking market is held in the grounds of the Moesgård Historical Museum near Århus. Traditional tournaments are held in Abenrå, Sønderborg and Gråsten on the first three weekends in July.

The events mentioned above constitute only a small fraction of Denmark's cultural calendar. The selection changes every year, and the Danish tourist office regularly publishes a *What's On* guide.

Food and Drink

Danish Cuisine

The names for the different meals in Denmark can often be rather confusing. *Morgenmad* is the 'morning meal', and is served in hotels and guest houses in the form of an opulent buffet, usually from 7–10am and sometimes until 11am. From noon until 2pm it's time for *frohkost*, which literally translated means breakfast but in reality is a light lunch. The main meal of the day is called *middag*, confusingly eaten between 6pm and 9pm. An alternative to a hot *middag* is a simpler *aftensmad*. Danish *hygge* (*see page 6*) also includes coffee and incredibly delicious cakes.

Traditional Danish fare is very substantial. Dishes featuring chicken, pork and fish are high on the list of popular favourites. The helpings are large, and are served with potatoes, thick gravy, red cabbage, gherkins or beetroot. Wholemeal food is growing increasingly popular, and is eaten in smaller portions. The supermarkets have very good fruit and vegetable departments.

As far as restaurants are concerned, the influence of French cuisine combined with magnificent seafood caught locally guarantees satisfaction for even the most fastidious gourmet. There's also a fine range of food to be had in somewhat cheaper establishments: the so-called 'Discount Restaurants' serve filling three-course meals for around Dkr50.

An increasingly frequent feature of the medium-priced restaurants is the 'all you can eat' style buffet; for around Dkr50–80 at lunchtime and Dkr100 at dinnertime. You can choose to eat Danish, Italian, Greek, Mongolian or Indian food. One recent fashion is the fondue – or grill-it-yourself restaurant. The price of an *à la carte* meal in the medium price category ranges between Dkr70 and Dkr150, while a menu with two to three courses in a high category restaurant will cost anywhere between Dkr200–300, and that's not including drinks.

Menus often have grilled, fried or baked specialities. Fish and beef tend to predominate: standard favourites include beefsteaks *(oksebøf)* and hamburgers *(hakkebøf)*, as well as salmon served in various ways.

One world-famous Danish culinary speciality is the legendary *smørrebrød*, which in many ways is a glorified sandwich. The list of 178 possible *smørrebrød* variations at one Copenhagen restaurant was 1.4m (5ft) long, and actually got into *The Guinness Book of Records*.

The principle is simple: the trick is how to put one together properly. Take a slice of rye bread and festoon it with large amounts of the following: shrimps, fried fish, small slices of pork or ham, salt beef, ox tongue or what-

Opposite: Welcoming smiles

A place to sample some Danish 'hygge'

Inviting display in Æroskøbing

ever. Then a second layer can be added at will from the list – capers, perhaps, or raw onion rings, anchovies, aspic, radish and horseradish slices. To crown it all, add a generous squirt of delicious mayonnaise. Three *smørrebrøds* – they usually cost Dkr15–50 a go – are usually enough to fill you up.

Ringing time in Ålborg

Smørrebrød is a typical *frokost* meal, but by no means the only one. The competition includes small, hot *(lune)* one-course meals and light salads. Baguettes, too, are getting more and more popular in city cafés; like the *smørrebrød* they, too, are piled high with layers of food.

Beer, Wine and Spirits

Denmark is the land of beer *(øl)*, and the many brands tend to arrive in bottles rather than on draught. Pilsener *(Tuborg grøn, Carlsberg Hof)* is the standard variety. Strong ales *(Guld Tuborg, Carlsberg Elefant)* are also very popular, but light beers and alcohol-free brands are growing increasingly fashionable *(Faxe free, Tuborg super light)*. The prices vary quite considerably, depending on the type of beer and the location of the pub.

Most restaurants will provide a good bottle of table wine for Dkr80–120, and dry varieties from France are very popular. Internationally well-known spirits are available from any bar, but among the best-known domestic products are *Aquavit* (the fiery Danish national drink, a caraway-flavoured *schnapps*) which is usually drunk very cold, and the bitter herbal *schnapps* known as *Gammel Dansk*. Both usually round off a meal, though *Gammel Dansk* is often drunk at breakfast time on public holidays.

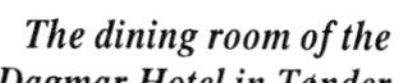

The dining room of the Dagmar Hotel in Tønder

Restaurant Selection

Copenhagen

A couple of good cafés to visit for lunch or dinner are **Zeze** and **Café Dan Turell** in Regnegade and **Krasnopolsky** in Vestergade, but you will easily find your own favourites.

For lunch try **Risotto** on Nytorv. Old-fashioned open sandwiches are served at **Café Sorgenfri** in Knabrostræde, at **Bjørnekælderen** at Frederiksberg Alle 55, and in many other bars; but the queen of *Smørrebrød* is **Ida Davidsen** at Store Kongensgade 70. One of the best cold buffets can be found at the **DSB Restaurant** in the Central Railway Station. **Den Sorte Ravn** is possibly the best (and most expensive) fish restaurant in town; the **Copenhagen Seafood Restaurant** at Oslo Plads 5 is also very good.

Some restaurants with attractive settings, good food and reasonable prices are **Peder Oxe** on Gråbrødretorv, the restaurant in **Nikolaj Church** on Nikolaj Plads, **Joanna** at Læderstræde 11 and **Din's** at Lille Kannikestræde 3. If you're willing to pay for high quality, visit **Lumskebugten** at Esplanaden 21 or **Els** in Store Strandstræde. Top-class gourmet cuisine can be enjoyed at **Kong Hans Kælder** at Vinggårdstræde 6.

Eating al fresco in Copenhagen

Århus

The best brunch in town can be had at **Café Englen** at Studsgade 3; those with larger appetites can make for the **Viking Bøthus** at Skolegade 10, which for the last 30 years has been famous for its speciality, 'Viking Casserole'. Nearby, at Skolegard 7, enjoy Danish food in great surroundings at the **Teater Bodega**; traditional fare can also be savoured at the **Radhuus Kaféen** along Sønder Alle and the **Restaurant Guldhornet** at Banegårdspladsen 10.

Stop at **Underground** (Nørregade 38 or in the pedestrian precinct), where they serve sandwiches, but the main attraction is ice cream.

Jacob's Bar BQ, in the courtyard of an old merchant's house at Vestergade 3, claims to be the first restaurant to bring the charcoal grill to Denmark. Vegetarians should visit **Husets Restaurant and Café** at Vester Alle 15. For an expensive but memorable culinary experience of home-made specialities, try **De 4 Årstider** at Åboulevarden 9.

Catering to all appetites in Århus

Ice cream Sunday

Odense

There are several good cafés in the area around **Brandt's Klæderfabrik**, and restaurant **Amfita** is just inside. **Café Birdy's** at Nørregade 21 is a nice combination café/restaurant and features vegetarian dishes.

Traditional Danish food is served in the **Sortebro Kro** at Sejerskovvej 20, **Den Gamle Kro** at Overgade 23 and at **Frank A** (Jernbanegade 4); next door to the latter is one of the city's best bars.

Recreation

A prize catch

Fishing

Fishing either out at sea or on the beach is free of charge after payment of an angling fee (Dkr100 per year) which can be paid at any post office or information bureau. A brochure issued by the tourist office mentions limitations (eg minimum size of the catch), where best to fish for what and also where to book deep-sea-fishing trips (Dkr100–400 depending on duration and region). Permits for fishing inland can generally be obtained from the nearest information bureau.

Teeing-off

Golf

Golf can be played on any of almost 100 different courses. Green fees vary a great deal, and are sometimes higher in the vicinity of Copenhagen. A round of golf on weekdays is also often cheaper than at weekends. Information can be obtained from the golfing brochure supplied by the Danish Tourist Office (*see page 92*).

Canoeing

Fans should head for the most popular region for longer tours: the lake region around Silkeborg and the upper reaches of the Gudenå as far as Randers (Jutland, *see page 39*). Another favourite, though smaller, region is around southern Sjælland along the Suså; also the lowland plain full of lakes with Lyngbysø, Bagsværdsø (international regatta route) and Furresø north of Copenhagen. Addresses of places where canoes can be hired and information on restrictions are obtainable from any information office.

Home on the range

Horse Riding

Horse riding is very popular in Denmark, and there are all kinds of activities available. It costs around Dkr80 an hour to rent a horse, and Dkr200 a day. Riding holidays with half board cost almost Dkr3000 a week. One-week-long riding tours across the Himmerland are also available, with tent accommodation (Ryttergaarden, Brøndum, DK-9500 Hobro, tel: 98 52 21 71). Other addresses obtainable from the Danish Tourist Office *(see page 92)*.

Swimming

Take care while swimming

Heading for the open sea

Swimming is possible almost anywhere along the coast (maps of safe bathing areas can be seen at most information offices).

A lot of places show the blue flag, which indicates that the water is clean, but these flags are becoming less popular. On supervised beaches, the flags will tell you whether bathing is safe or not (red = strictly no bathing; yellow = bathing may be dangerous; green = safe bathing). Generally speaking, great care should be taken when swimming in the North Sea and children should be supervised at all times.

Sailing and Surfing

These and other water sports are extremely popular in Denmark because of the steady, strong wind and the variable conditions. Some islands and strips of coastline have been designated as bird or seal sanctuaries and are closed to surfers and sailors. It's important to know exactly where these are, because the fines for trespassing are high. The country has around 200 harbours for hobby yachtsmen.

Klitmøller on the North Sea coast near Thisted is considered one of the best windsurfing areas in Europe but, as with all North Sea areas, you need to know exactly what you're doing. The Baltic is less of a strain, though, as are the Limfjord or Ringkøbing Fjord. Almost 40 windsurfing schools can teach beginners. The Danish Tourist Office has special brochures on sailing and windsurfing.

Tennis

This can be played at several hotels, holiday parks and campsites. Information offices also provide court times at clubs or in halls.

Walking

There are suggested routes for every region of the country available from the Forestry Protection Office. These can also be obtained from local information offices. Long-distance routes are gradually being introduced too, especially coastal routes in various parts of Jutland, around Bornholm and along the Isefjord in northern Sjælland.

HOTEL DAGMAR
HOTEL RESTAURANT
VÆGTER
KÆLDEREN

Getting There

Opposite: Dagmar Hotel

By Plane

There are daily flights to Copenhagen from most European countries and North America, as well as the Far East. International traffic also serves the airport at Billund in west-central Jutland. The national carrier is SAS, Scandinavian Airlines System, for international traffic, and DANAIR (consisting of Maersk Air, SAS and Cimber Air) serves most domestic routes.

Copenhagen's Kastrup Airport is the hub for Denmark's domestic flights. Allow yourself 45 minutes for any change from international to domestic (or vice versa). Ten domestic airports are regularly served from Kastrup. Flights last from 40 to 60 minutes. There are 50 percent reductions for children aged between 2 and 11, and no charge for children under 2.

Special fares with special conditions (minimum length of stay, alteration restrictions) can make domestic flights a lot cheaper:

– *Rød-pris* (red price) = 50 percent discount outside peak times on workdays. Also applies to children.

– *Grøn-pris* (green price) = roughly 30 percent discount on single and return flights for individuals, and between 60 and 70 percent for family members at weekends.

– Standby tickets available for those under 25 years of age.

– During peak season (end-June–mid-August) there are several last-minute special offers available. Nearly every Danish town has an SAS or a DANAIR office; reservations can also be made at any SAS office or good travel agents in the UK and US.

By Car/ferry

Jutland and Fyn can be reached from Germany via the motorway border post at Flensburg (autobahn A7/E45). The section of the E45 that travels north as far as Ålborg was completed in 1994; near Kolding the E20 branches off in the direction of Fyn. Another way of entering Denmark from Germany is via Niebüll and Tønder (*see Route 2*), though the roads tend to be very overcrowded here in peak season – and especially on Saturdays, when the holiday cottages change hands.

Sjælland, Lolland, Falster and Møn (*see Route 11*) can be comfortably reached from German ports via the E47 (Hamburg – Puttgarden – ferry – Rødby) or via the E55 (Berlin – Rostock – Warnemünde – ferry – Gedser).

Visitors from the UK have the option of taking the ferry to Esbjerg in West Jutland (*see Route 8*) – there are regular services from Harwich and, during the summer months, from Newcastle.

The journey begins

Watch out for cyclists

Getting Around

By Car

The 3,535km/2,196 mile long **Daisy Route** (marked by road signs showing a daisy on a brown background) leads tourists to sights the length and breadth of the country. Though indicating places of great interest and variety, the daisy signs do not guarantee fast progress. A route map in English can be obtained from most tourist information offices (*see page 93*), as well as from the Danish Tourist Office (*see page 92*).

Traffic regulations: Speed limits: on motorways 110kmph (68mph), on other roads 80kmph (49mph), in built-up areas 50kmph (31mph), and lorries and cars with trailers or caravans are allowed to travel no faster than 70kmph (43mph). The maximum alcohol level allowed is 80 millilitres. Headlights have to stay on all day. A sequence of white triangles painted on the road before intersections means 'Give Way'. While driving in Denmark it is important to avoid the smaller side-roads whenever possible, because these tend to be frequented by cyclists, many of whom are families with children.

Yellow kerbstone markings signify 'No Parking', and are usually reinforced by road-signs. The times printed in black mean Monday to Friday (Saturday), and the red ones Sunday and public holidays. Parking discs are needed in some areas with limited parking, and these can be obtained from banks, information offices and filling stations

The Danish Automobile Club (FDM) has no breakdown service, but the private breakdown service known as Falck has over 100 stations across the country. Numbers are listed in the local phone books. Breakdown service needs to be paid for immediately.

Accidents: Foreign car insurance companies are represented in Denmark by Dansk Forening for international Motorkøretojsforsikring, Amaliegade 10, DK-1256 København, tel: 33 13 75 55. This is the number to ring if a foreign car has been either partially or fully responsible for an accident.

Easy riders

By Bicycle

Cycle routes are extremely well-marked in Denmark (the sign to look out for is a white bicycle on a blue background, which usually also shows the route number and the distance in kilometres). There are 10 national cycle routes (covering a total of 3,300km/2,050 miles) right across the country, supplemented by several thousand kilometres of local routes.

Guides in English to all parts of the country with detailed maps are available from information offices in Denmark and bookshops. With only a few exceptions, bicycles can be taken on trains in Denmark, and on regional buses too, provided there is enough room. For information on routes and practical advice, contact: Dansk Cyklistforbund (Danish Cyclists' Association), Rømersgade 7, 1362 Copenhagen K, tel: 33 32 31 21.

By Bus

Inside Denmark there are several long-distance bus routes, eg between Copenhagen and towns in Jutland, between Odense and Gedser via Langeland/Lolland and between Copenhagen and the Bornholm ferry docks in the Swedish town of Ystad. The regional buses within Denmark provide discount tickets for tourists and also special offers that include transport and admission to sights.

By Rail

Fredericia is the name of the central rail junction in Denmark with connecting routes to all parts of the country.

Trains are regular and frequent within Denmark itself. This also applies to services connecting Sjælland and Jutland via Fyn across the new Great Belt Fixed Link. Night trains are few and far between, however.

All seats on trains from Copenhagen to Jutland via the Great Belt have to be reserved in advance. Some regional and local trains only have 2nd class. The precision of the trains, bus and ferry timetables is admirable.

Train ticket prices are based on a zone system which also includes a few ferry routes.

If you buy your train ticket in Denmark, there are several special offers available:

- Tuesday, Wednesday, Thursday and Saturday (public holidays excluded) are 'cheap days' (up to 20 percent reduction).
- Children, the elderly (65 and over), small groups and holders of student cards always travel more cheaply.
- Excursions to sights, amusement parks and interesting towns are sold as package deals (admission fees included).

Trains are regular and frequent

By Boat

The special ferry brochure from the Danish Tourist Office (*see page* 92) lists around 50 ferry connections within Denmark itself and another 20 cross-border ones every year. Ferry reservations are mostly made by phone: callers are given a reservation number and have to show it at the docks as proof of booking. Otherwise, any good travel agent can make reservations and issue tickets. Booking is not possible, however, for a lot of short trips. Car drivers usually need to be at the docks around 15 minutes before departure, though sometimes 30 minutes or even an hour can be advisable on popular routes.

All aboard!

Discussing priorities

Facts for the Visitor

Travel documents

Anyone arriving in Denmark needs a passport, valid for a minimum of three months. Tourist visas are not required for citizens of the European Union, Canada and the United States. Citizens of other nationalities should check with a Danish embassy or consulate before departure.

Customs regulations

Visitors to Denmark may bring in an unlimited number of items for personal use (sport, camping, photographic equipment, etc). There are limitations on only a few imported goods bought in EU countries: 1.5 litres of spirits, and 300 cigarettes or 75 cigars or 400g tobacco. The regulations governing the import of goods from outside the EU are stricter: 1 litre of spirits, 2 litres of wine, 200 cigarettes or 50 cigars or 250g tobacco, 50g perfume or 250ml Eau de Toilette; 0.5kg coffee; 100g tea; and other goods to a maximum value of Dkr350 (roughly $50).

Information

In the UK: The Danish Tourist Board, 55 Sloane Street, London SW1X 9SY, tel: 0171 259 5959.
In the US: The Danish Tourist Board, 6555 Third Avenue, 18th floor, New York, NY 10017, tel: 212 949 2333 or 2322; Scandinavian Tourist Board, 150 North Michigan Avenue, Suite 2110, Chicago, Il 60601, tel: 312 726 1120; Scandinavian Tourist Board, 8929 Wiltshire Boulevard, Beverly Hills, CA 90211, tel: 213 854 1549.

In Copenhagen: Information is available from Københavns Turistinformation, Bernstorffsgade 1, 1577 København V, tel: 33 11 13 25, fax: 33 93 49 69. For hotel reservations, tel: 33 12 28 80.

There are local information offices in the larger towns and in all tourist areas. Many tourist areas have radio stations that transmit tourist information, tips and news about events in English; the frequencies and transmission times can be obtained from the local information offices.

Nude bathing

Nude bathing is officially limited to a few stretches of beach, but is being increasingly tolerated. Women can go topless on any beach, but T-shirts are generally worn at bars, restaurants and shops close to the beach.

Flags

There's hardly a holiday home in Denmark without a flagpole. According to law, only the flags of Denmark, the other Scandinavian countries and the European Union can be flown. Those hoisting an illegal flag (eg the British one) must expect a visit from the police. There's no fine for first-time offenders, but the flag does have to be promptly lowered.

Strictly Danish

Currency and exchange

The unit of currency in Denmark is the Danish krone, plural kroner, abbreviated to Dkr, and made up of 100 øre. Banknotes have denominations of Dkr50, Dkr100, Dkr500 and Dkr1000, and there are 1, 2, 5 10 and 20 kroner coins, and also 25 and 50 øre (øre amounts not payable in cash are rounded off, but remain the same on cheques, etc).

Money exchange (there's a fee!) is possible in banks (Monday to Friday 9.30am–4pm, Thursday until 6pm) and at some currency exchange offices (usually open till around 10pm). The maximum amount payable by Eurocheque is Dkr1500; and traveller's cheques are also widely accepted. Visa and MasterCard are accepted in most shops. American Express cards can be used in major hotels and shops, but, in general, are not very popular.

Colourful wares

Opening times

Opening times in Denmark are quite flexible, and the times given here are just a rough guide. Shops are open Monday to Friday 9am–5.30pm, some staying open as late as 8pm (Friday evening is usually the latest); closing for lunch (noon–2pm) is most common in the countryside, and increasingly rare in the city. Shops close between noon and 2pm on Saturday, and on the first Saturday in the month between 4pm and 5pm. Bakeries, kiosks with a broad range of goods on sale and shops in tourist areas tend to stay open very late, and are also open on Sunday. The minimarkets at some filling stations also have an assortment of basic goods, as do several campsites and holiday parks.

Souvenirs

Royal Copenhagen Porcelain

Classic souvenirs include Royal Copenhagen Porcelain, glass by Holmegård, and jewellery or cutlery by silversmith Georg Jensen. More popular as souvenirs, mainly because they are cheaper, are craft goods such as ceramics, studio glass, processed emeralds or candles; many of the workshops are situated in tourist areas. Numerous antique dealers have also set up shop in these regions, and they often have some very good bargains.

By no means cheap, but very popular, are products famous for their streamlined, classical elegance and Danish design: household goods, furniture, and also high-quality stereo and TV equipment.

VAT reclamation

Part of the reason for the high prices in Danish shops is a value-added tax (called MOMS) of 22 percent added to all goods and services. Visitors can avoid making this contribution to the Danish state by having their purchase shipped home. Shops that cater to tourists know about these services, and will provide information about the procedures. If you buy something and want to take it with you immediately, look for a sign saying 'Danish Tax–Free Shopping'. About 1,500 shops are members of this association, and the VAT spent in them will be refunded on departure from Denmark.

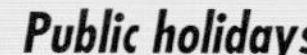

Public holidays

New Year's Day, Good Friday, Ascension, Whitsun, Christmas and New Year's Eve are all public holidays; also Maundy Thursday (the Thursday before Easter), which is a church holiday, and the afternoon of 5 June, which is Constitution Day. Many shops close at noon on 1 May too.

Postage

Post your cards here

The price for sending postcards or ordinary letters anywhere to Northern or Western Europe is the same (at the moment Dkr3.75). A large 'A' needs to be drawn next to the stamp, or a blue sticker saying 'A-Prioritaire' needs to be affixed. If letters are handed in at a post office the cheaper and slower 'B-Economique' method can be chosen (better value if the letter is heavy).

Telephone

International calls are possible from all phones. There are numerous public telephones that take coins or cards, but they all look very different (minimum charge for calls abroad: Dkr2–5 depending on region). Phone cards for Dkr20, Dkr50 or Dkr100 are available at post office shops, kiosks and post offices.

To make an international call, lift the receiver, insert the money (if necessary), dial 00 then the country code, followed by the area code (omitting any initial 0) and the number required.

AT&T, tel: 800-1-0010. SPRINT, tel: 800-1-0877, other credit cards, tel: 800-1-0022

It's also possible to get rung back at phone boxes in Denmark: the number is usually on the phone itself or on the operating instructions sign. The code for Denmark for callers from England is 01045 and then the eight-digit number. Denmark has no area codes.

Electricity

220 volts AC. Visitors are advised to bring adaptors.

Tipping

Service is included in hotel and restaurant bills. Tips are an acknowledgement of good service, and the general rule is: you don't have to, but you can if you like. The same applies to taxis.

You can tip if you like

Medical assistance and health insurance

Health care is generally free in Denmark. Acute illness or accidents will be treated at the emergency room of the nearest hospital. Members of the EU who are properly insured can receive the same amount of free medical treatment as any Dane if they have a EU medical insurance card E111 (obtainable from the Department of Health). Be prepared to pay a high percentage of dental bills yourself, however. Some medicines are not be covered either. Visitors from outside the EU should insure they have the necessary medical cover before departure.

Emergencies

The number to ring in the event of any emergency is 112 (toll-free).

Facilities for the Disabled

Most public buildings and several museums have facilities for the disabled, eg wheelchair ramps, widened doorways, etc. The same applies to the newer hotels, youth hostels, holiday parks and campsites; older buildings are being increasingly modernised. The Danish Tourist Office brochure *Travelling in Denmark for the Disabled* lists suitable accommodation.

Diplomatic Representation

British Embassy, Kaftlevej 36–40, 2100 Copenhagen 0, tel: 35 26 46 000.

US Embassy, Dag Hammarskjölds Allé 24, 2100 Copenhagen 0, tel: 31 42 31 44.

There are many accommodation alternatives

Accommodation

Denmark is to be considered a country of holiday homes first and foremost. Alternatives include not only campsites but also city hotels, palace hotels, private accommodation (bed & breakfast), double rooms or family rooms in youth hostels (*see page 102*), or island camps.

Bed & Breakfast can be organised at most information offices, and is a relatively economical accommodation option especially in the city. In Copenhagen it's worth looking around outside the city limits; the information office in the northern suburb of Lyngby can organise several private rooms, and transport to the city is very good from this area.

Camping, caravanning and camping huts. Almost 50 percent of Denmark's 550 campsites stay open during the winter months. Many have toilet and water facilities for caravans and motor homes. On campsites, huts are being rented out increasingly often, providing occupants with a solid roof over their heads while enabling access to all the usual facilities.

Since 1994, officially recognised campsites have been graded into five price categories, and prices vary accordingly. A camping pass is always needed; they can be bought for a small annual fee at all campsites. The International Camping Card is also accepted. Camping away from official sites or spending the night in one's car is not allowed.

The Danish Tourist Office (*see page 92*) has a great deal of material on camping (lists of all the sites, etc).

Holiday homes can be anything from small wooden huts sleeping four people to luxury homes sleeping ten or more, complete with their own private swimming pools. Bedding is always supplied.

Prices vary depending on the decor, the location and also the time of stay. The same house can cost over 50 percent more in peak season. Generally speaking, the most expensive and most luxurious holiday homes are along the west coast of Jutland; houses on Bornholm are also relatively expensive. Out of peak season, a normal house can still be had for as little as £120 a week; a luxury home on the North Sea coast can easily cost £1000 a week, and sometimes even more. The Danish Tourist Office publishes the addresses of numerous Danish holiday home letting companies every year. Houses can also be booked from abroad; this may cost a little more than renting a house on the spot, but there's also the comfort of knowing that a proper contract exists.

Farmhouse holidays come in two versions: room and board (usually half-board) or self-catering apartments. Local specialists for farmhouse holidays include Bondegårdferie, c/o Horsens Turistbureau, Søndergade 26, DK-8700 Horsens, tel: 70 10 41 20, fax: 75 60 21 90; and Landsforeningen for Landboturisme, Leresvej 2, DK-8410 Rønde, tel: 86 37 39 00, fax: 86 37 35 50.

Island camps (*Ø-lejr*). Every summer camps are set up on several of the smaller islands according to various activities (eg music and dance), or certain target audiences in the alternative scene. Cooking and sleeping takes place in communal tents. For more information contact Ø-lejr Kontoret, Vendersgade 8, DK-1363 København K, tel: 33 11 55 81.

Hotels and country inns (Kroer). Ordinary rooms in hotels and country inns can still be found outside Copenhagen for prices of Dkr250 or less (per person in double room with breakfast), and good rooms for Dkr325. Prices change according to season in the holiday regions, but hotels only a few miles out of town that usually specialise in accommodation for conferences and congresses often have cheap offers in the summer months and at weekends. Try: Best Western hotels (central reservations: Vodroffsvej 44, DK-1900 Frederiksberg C, tel: 31 39 39 27, fax: 31 39 51 08) and Scandic Hotels (Kettevej 4, DK-2650 Hvidovre, tel: 36 77 70 00, fax: 37 77 50 77).

Far from the madding crowd

Two cheaper types of hotel are the Missionhotels and the new Discounthotels, eg the Cab Inns in Copenhagen which have rooms like ships' cabins, with beds that have to be made by the occupants themselves.

Kroer (singular: *kro*) are country inns that can be found along the most important traffic routes and in the smaller towns. A lot of *kroer* have excellent rooms and fine food. The designation *kro* is not copyrighted, however, and so standards can vary. Establishments run by the Dansk Kro Ferie organisation are all good, as are the more traditional *kongelig privilegerede Kroer*. Details from: Dansk Kroferie, Søndergade 31, DK 8700 Horsens, Denmark, tel: 75 62 35 44, fax: 75 62 38 72.

Castles and Manor Houses. Several castles and manor houses in Denmark have been turned into comfortable hotels, and can be a very sophisticated, if rather expensive way of spending a holiday here. However, over a dozen of the best castle hotels have joined forces and alongside package deals (accommodation plus banquet) they also provide 'castle stay vouchers'. More information from Dansk Slotte og Herregårde, Fælledvej 11B, DK-8800 Viborg, tel: 86 60 38 44, fax: 86 60 38 31.

The Dronninglund Slot Hotel, a converted castle

Here is a list of selected hotels for the various destinations and routes covered in this guide. $$$$ means luxury, $$$ expensive, $$ medium-priced and $ cheap.

The Copenhagen Admiral

Copenhagen: $$$$**Hotel d'Angleterre**, Komgens Nytorv 34, 1050 København K, tel: 33 12 00 95 – the most traditional luxury hotel in the country; **SAS Royal Copenhagen**, Hammerichgade 1, 1611 København V, tel: 33 14 14 12 – modern and luxurious; $$$**Copenhagen Admiral**, Tolboldgade 24–28, 1253 København K, tel: 33 11 82 82 – right at the harbour; **Webers Hotel**, Vesterbrogade 11b, 1620 København V, tel: 31 31 14 32; $$**Hotel Cosmopole**, Colbjømsensgade 5–11, 1652 København V, tel: 31 21 33 33; **Scandic Bell Air**, Løjtegaardsvej 99, 2770 Kastrup, tel: 31 51 30 33 – near the airport; **Scandic Hotel København/Hoje Taastrup**, Carl Gustav Gade 1, 2630 Tåstrup, tel: 42 99 77 66; $**Ibsens Hotel**, Vendersgade 23, 1363 København K, tel: 33 13 19 16 – very good value, central, and comfortable too; **Hotel Cap Inn**, Danasvej 32–34, 1910 Frederiksbjerg, tel: 31 21 04 00; **Hotel Cap Inn Scandinavia**, Vodroffsvej 57, 1900 Frederiksberg, tel: 35 36 11 11.

Odense: $$$$**Hotel Hans Christian Andersen**, Claus Bergs Gade 7, tel: 66 14 78 00 – modern hotel with congress facilities plus casino; $$$**Odense Plaza**, Østre Stationsvej 24, tel: 66 11 77 45 – traditional establishment with good food; $**Missionshotel Ansgar**, Østre Stationsvej 32, tel: 66 11 96 93.

Ålborg: $$$$**Hvide Hus**, Vesterbro 2, tel: 98 13 84 00 – modern hotel at congress centre; **Scheelsminde**, Scheelsmindevej 35, 9100 Ålborg, tel: 98 18 32 33 – a former mansion; **Scandic**, Hadsundvej 200, 9220 Ålborg Øst, tel:

98 15 45 00 – modern hotel on the outskirts; $$**Prinsens Hotel**, Prinsengade 14–16, tel: 98 13 37 33 – fully renovated hotel in town.

Århus: $$$$**Royal**, Store Torv 4, tel: 86 12 00 11 – centrally located with a casino; $$$**Marselis**, Strandvejen 25, tel: 86 14 44 11 – magnificent location on the bay outside town; $$**Missionshotel Ansgar**, Banegårdsplads 14, tel: 86 12 41 22 – centrally located near the station; $**Eriksens Hotel**, Banegårdsplads 6–8, tel: 86 13 62 96 – simple town hotel.

Royal Hotel , the casino

Route 2. Tønder: $$**Tønderhus**, Jomfruestien 1, tel: 74 72 22 22 – cheap family hotel. **Ribe:** $$$**Hotel Dagmar**, Torvet 1, tel: 75 42 00 33 – the oldest hotel in Denmark, built in 1581 and quite unique; $$**Den Gamle Arrest**, Torvet 11, tel: 75 42 37 00 – used to be a prison; **Weis' Stue**, Torvet 2, tel: 75 42 07 00 – in a half-timbered house dating from 1600. **Hanstholm:** $$$**Golfhotel Hanstholm**, Byvej 2, tel: 97 69 19 44 – luxurious, some rooms have a sea view; $**Hanstholm Sømandshjem**, Kai Lindbergsgade 71, tel: 97 96 11 45 – for a real dose of harbour atmosphere. **Hjørring:** $$$**Phønix**, Jernbanegade 6, tel: 98 92 54 55 – centrally located hotel. **Hirtshals:** $$$**Skaga Hotel**, Willemosevej 1, tel: 98 94 55 00 – modern and very well-equipped; $$**Hotel Hirtshals**, Havnegade 2, tel: 98 94 20 77 – centrally located with view of harbour. **Skagen:** $$$**Brøndums Hotel**, Anchersvej 3, tel: 98 44 15 55 – once the meeting-place for the Skagen painters and now an institution; **Skagen Hotel**, Gl Landevej 39, tel: 98 44 22 33 – holiday hotel in the south next to dunes and forests; $$**Petit**, Holstvej 4, tel: 98 44 11 99 – centrally located; $**Skagen Sømandshjem**, Østre Strandvej 2, tel: 98 44 25 88 – cheap and centrally located near the harbour.

Hotel Dagmar bedroom

Route 4. Frederikshavn: $$$**Stena Hotel**, Tordenskjoldsgade 14, tel: 98 43 32 33 – luxurious; $$**Hotel 1987**, Havnegade 8e, tel: 98 43 19 87 – centrally located tourist hotel; **Aktivitel**, Knivholtvej, tel: 98 43 23 77 – modern sport hotel near golf course. **Læsø (Byrum):** $$**Nygaard**, Østerbyvejen, 9940 Byrum, tel: 98 49 16 66. **Dronninglund:** $$$**Dronninglund Slot**, Slotsgade 8, tel: 98 84 33 00. **Hobro:** $$**Bramslevgaard Herregårdspension**, Bramslev Bakker 4, tel: 98 51 20 30 – on an estate west of the town. **Randers:** $$$**Randers Hotel**, Torvegade 1, tel: 86 42 34 22 – just a few steps from the town hall; **Scandic Hotel Kongens Ege**, Gl Hadsundvej 2, tel: 86 43 03 00 – well-located, for businessmen, good summer rates. **Skanderborg:** $$**Slotskroen**, Adelgade 23, tel: 86 52 00 12 – good family hotel in renovated *kro*. **Horsens:** $$$**Skandic Hotel Bygholm Park**, Schuttesvej 6, tel:

Inside the Dronninglund Slot

Jorgensens Hotel

75 62 23 33 – well-located on outskirts; $$**Jørgensens Hotels**, Søndergade 17, tel: 75 62 16 00. **Vejle:** $$$**Munkebjerg**, Munkebjergvej 125, tel: 75 72 35 00 – great location above fjord, with casino; **Scandic Hotel Australia**, Dæmningen 6, tel: 75 82 43 11 – first class hotel with good tourist rates; $**Grejsdalens Hotel & Kro**, Greisdalsvej 384, tel: 75 85 30 04 – small and simple, amid natural scenery some way out of town. **Kolding:** $$$**Scanticon**, Skovbrynet, tel: 75 50 15 55 – luxury hotel with good weekend and summer rates; **Scandic**, Kokholm 2, tel: 75 51 77 00 – modern business hotel; $$**Saxildhus**, Banegårdspladsen, tel: 75 52 12 00 – family hotel not far from pedestrian precinct. **Haderslev:** $$$**Norden**, Storegade 55, tel: 74 52 40 30 – first-class hotel, centrally located. **Åbenrå:** $$$**Hotel Europa**, HP Hansensgade 10, tel: 74 62 26 22 – central hotel, comfortable; $**Sølyst Kro**, Flensborgvej 164, Styrtum, tel: 74 62 11 63 – guest-house to the south by the sea.

Route 6. Rømø: $$$**Hotel Færgegården**, Vestergade 1–5, tel: 74 75 54 32 – thatched house, formerly a captain's cottage. **Mageltønder:** $$**Schackenburg Slotskro**, Slotsgaden 42, tel: 74 73 83 83. **Sønderborg:** $$**Scandic Sønderborg**, Rosengade, tel: 74 42 19 00 – excellent location near beach, castle and pedestrian precinct.

Legoland

Route 7. Esbjerg: $$$**Britannia**, Torvet, tel: 75 13 01 11 – modern hotel in the centre; $$**Scandic Olympic**, Strandbygade 3, tel: 75 18 11 88 – modern hotel at western end of pedestrian precinct; $**Hotel Hjerting**, Strandpromenaden 1, tel: 75 11 52 44 – traditional hotel 8km (5 miles) north of centre on Hjerting beach. **Fanø (Nordby):** $$$**Nordby Kro**, Strandvejen 12, tel: 75 16 35 89 – 300-year-old *kro* with superb restaurant and just four rooms. **Fredericia:** $$$**Kronprinds Frederik**, Vestre Ringvej 96, tel: 75 91 00 00 – luxury hotel with good summer rates. **Jelling:** $**Jelling Kro**, Gormsgade 16, tel: 75 87 10 06 – comfortable *kro* close to major sights. **Billund:** $$**Propelleren**, Nordmarksvej 8, tel: 75 33 81 33 – good hotel close to Legoland; $**Motel Svanen**, Nordmarksvej 8, tel: 75 33 28 33 – only a short walk to Legoland.

Route 8. Ringkøbing: $$$**Fjordgården**, Vesterkær 28, tel: 97 32 14 00 – excellent family hotel with good food. **Herning:** $$$**Eyde**, Torvet 1, tel: 97 22 18 00 – traditional hotel in the centre with good food. **Silkeborg:** $$$**Dania**, Torvet 5, tel: 86 82 01 11 – traditional hotel in the centre; $$**Scandic Silkeborg**, Udgårdsvej 2, tel: 86 80 35 33 – modern hotel with lake view; **Gammel Rye Kro**, Ryesgade 8, 8680 Ry, tel: 86 89 80 42 – country inn with substantial cooking near the Himmelbjerg.

Route 9. Middelfart: $$$**Kongebrogaarden**, Indevej 2, tel: 64 41 11 22 – modern and comfortable hotel right next to the water with view of Little Belt and bridges; $$**Hindsgavl Slot**, Hindsgavl Allé 7, tel: 64 41 88 00 – castle and conference hotel. **Nyborg:** $$$$**Hesselet**, Christianslundvej 119, tel: 65 31 30 29 – top hotel in 60s style, right on the sea; $$$**Nyborg Strand**, Østerøvej 2, tel: 65 31 31 31 – congress hotel right on the Great Belt, lower summer rates. **Fåborg:** $$**Færgegaarden**, Christian IX Vej 31, tel: 62 61 11 15 – hotel in old part of Fåborg with good food. **Tåsinge (Troense):** $$**Hotel Troense**, Strandgade 5–7, tel: 62 22 54 12 – small hotel with view of the Sound. **Langeland (Rudkøbing):** $$$**Skudehavn**, Havnegade 21, tel: 62 51 46 00 – hotel and holiday park with own marina; $$**Humble Hotel**, Ristingevej 2, 5932 Humble, tel: 62 57 11 34 12 – village hotel in south of Langeland. **Kerteminde:** $$**Tornøes Hotel**, Strandgade 5, tel: 65 32 16 05 – traditional hotel near the harbour. **Ærø (Ærøskøbing):** $$**Ærøhus**, Vestergade 38, tel: 62 52 10 03 – traditional hotel in old part of town; $**Dunkær Kro**, Dunkærvej 1, tel: 62 52 15 54 – country inn with great food. **Ærø (Marstal):** $$$**Ærø Strand**, Egehovedvej 4 – beach hotel.

The delights of Ærø

Route 11A. Rødbyhavn: $$**Danhotel**, Havnegade 2, tel: 54 60 53 66 – modern hotel near ferry harbour. **Maribo:** $$$**Hvide Hus**, Vestergade, tel: 53 88 10 11 – modern hotel by a lake with good summer rates. **Gedser:** $$$**Nørrevang**, Marielyst Strandvej 32, 4873-Marielyst, tel: 54 13 62 62 – very good hotel near beach, superb restaurant. **Nykøbing F.:** $$$**Falster**, Skovalléen, tel: 54 85 93 93 – modern hotel, well-situated. **Vordingborg:** $$**Kong Valdemar,** Algade 101, tel: 53 77 00 95. **Køge:** $$$**Hvide Hus**, Strandvejen 111, tel: 53 65 36 90 – modern hotel just 100m (300ft) from the beach; **Niels Juel**, Toldbodvej 20, tel: 56 63 18 00 – new hotel, centrally located near harbour.

The charms of Køge

Route 11B. Korsør: $$$**Tårnborg Parkhotel**, Ørnumvej 6, tel: 58 35 01 10 – modern conference hotel in park outside town. **Sorø:** $$$**Sorø Storkro**, Abildvej 1, tel: 53 63 56 00 – modern *kro* with unusual thatched roof; $$**Postgarden**, Storgade 27, tel: 53 63 22 22 – centrally located hotel with long tradition. **Ringsted:** $$$**Sørup Herregaard**, Sørupvej 26, tel: 53 64 30 02 – mansion in park south of town, with excellent cuisine; **Scandic Ringsted**, Nørretory 57, tel: 53 61 93 00 – modern business-class hotel with reasonable summer rates. **Jystrup:** $$**Skjoldenæsholm Hotel**, Skjoldenæsvej 106, tel: 53 62 81 04 – in a neoclassical mansion. **Roskilde:** $$$**Prindsen**, Algade 12, tel: 42 35 80 10 – elegant town hotel, the most central of all.

Route 11C. Næstved: $$$**Vinhuset**, Skt Peders Kirkeplads 4, tel: 53 72 08 07 – stylish hotel with 200 years of tradition and a good wine-cellar, centrally located. **Helsingør:** $$$**Scanticon Borupgaard**, Nørrevej 80, 3070 Snekkersten, tel: 42 22 03 33 – first-class hotel in a park. **Hundested:** $$**Hundested Kro og Hotel**, Nørregade 10, tel: 42 33 75 38 – centrally located inn, great seafood. **Kalundborg:** $$**Ole Lunds Gård**, Krokodilgade 1–3, tel: 53 51 01 65 – in the pedestrian precinct.

Route 11D. Møn (Borre): $$$**Liselund Slot**, Langebjergvej 6, 4791 Borre, tel: 55 81 20 81 – a romantic hotel in a villa next to the castle. **Kelby:** $$**Præstekilde Kro & Hotel**, Klintevej 116, 4780 Kelby, tel: 55 81 34 43 – a good *kro* at the centre of Møn, east of Stege. **Naksov:** $$**Skovridergaarden**, Svingelen 4, tel: 53 92 03 55 – nice hotel in a wood outside the town.

Beautiful Bornholm

Bornholm: $$$**Friheden**, Tejnvej 80, 3770 Allinge-Sandkaas, tel: 56 48 04 25 – ecological family hotel near beach; **Fredensborg**, Strandvejen 116, 3700 Rønne, tel: 56 95 44 44 – modern hotel south of Rønne, near the sea; $$**Pension Slægtsgården**, Østergade 3, 3770 Allinge, tel: 56 48 17 42 – family-run boarding-house in a half-timbered courtyard in picturesque Allinge old town.

Samsø: $$**Nordby Kro**, Hovedgaden 8, 8305 Nordby, tel: 86 59 60 86 – country *kro* with good food; **Ballen Hotel**, Avej 21, 8305 Ballen – hotel near the beach in Ballen on island's east coast.

Youth and Family Hostels

Youth hostels in Denmark are known as *Vandrerhjem* ('wanderers' home') and it's clear from the name that not only 'youth' has access. There are no age limits.

Most of the establishments have double rooms or family rooms, often with shower and WC; there are no strict rules on closing times in the evening. Almost all the establishments have self-catering facilities, but also serve substantial and good-value meals.

The Danish Tourist Office does a list of all hostels (*see page 92*), and further information is available from Landsforeningen Danmarks Vandrerhjem, Vesterbrogade 39, DK-1620 København V, tel: 31 31 36 12, fax: 31 31 36 26.

Here is a list of some hostels:

Copenhagen: Vejlands Allé 200, 2300 København S – 144 family rooms.

Odense: Kragsbjergvej 121, tel: 66 13 04 25 – idyllic half-timbered building, 20 family rooms.

Århus: Pavillonen, Marienlundvej 10, DK-8240 Risskov, tel: 86 16 72 98 – nicely located in a forest.

Route 2. Hjørring: Thomas Morildsvej 11, tel: 98 92 67 00; **Hirtshals:** Hirtshals Wandrerhjem, Kystvejen 53, tel: 98 94 12 48 – near lighthouse and beach, some family rooms; **Læsø:** Lækevej 6, 9950 Vesterø Havn, tel: 98 49 91 95 – the only hostel on the island near the ferry docks.

Route 4. Randers: Gethersvej 1, tel: 86 42 50 44 – hostel with 30 family rooms; **Skanderborg:** Dyrehaven 9, tel: 86 52 06 73 – hostel in fine scenery on the edge of Skanderborger Sø, with 33 family rooms; **Horsens:** Flintebakken 150, tel: 75 61 67 77 – on edge of conservation area north of centre, with 27 family rooms; **Haderslev:** Erlevhus, Erlevvej 34, tel: 74 52 13 47 – hostel on Haderslev Dam with 30 family rooms.

Route 6. Rømø: Poppelgården, Lyngvejen 7, Havneby, tel: 74 75 51 88 – hostel with thatched roof, 25 family rooms; **Sønderborg:** Kærvej 70, tel: 74 42 56 31 – modern hostel with 300 beds and 34 family rooms.

Most youth hostels have family rooms

Route 8. Herning: Holingknuden 2, tel: 97 12 31 44 – this hostel (built 1993) has 28 well-equipped family rooms.

Route 9. Svendborg: Vestergade 45, tel: 62 21 66 99; **Kerteminde:** Skovvej 46, tel: 65 32 39 29 – hostel with 30 good family rooms in the middle of a wood.

Route 11. Nykøbing F.: Østre Allé 110, tel: 54 85 66 99 – hostel with 22 family rooms; **Korsør:** Svalegarden, Tovesvej 30F, tel: 53 57 10 22 – nice hostel with 27 family rooms; **Roskilde:** Hørgården, Hørhusene 61, tel: 42 35 21 84 – on the western edge of town, with 21 family rooms. **Helsingør:** Villa Moltke, Ndr. Strandvej 24, tel: 49 21 16 40 – in a mansion, near the water, and with 36 family rooms; **Tisvildeleje:** Sankt Helene Center, Bygmarken 30, tel: 42 30 98 50 – hostel in modern holiday park with 40 family rooms (huts also available); **Nykøbing Sjælland:** Ånneberg, Egebjergvej 162, tel: 59 93 00 62 – hostel in renovated mansion with own beach, 14 family rooms, in a large park; **Kalundborg:** Stadtion Allé 5, tel: 599 56 13 66 – a modern 'luxury' hostel with 28 family rooms.

Bornholm marina

Bornholm: Skt Jørgens Gård, 3760 Gudhjem, tel: 56 48 50 35 – lively hostel with 25 family rooms.

Samsø: Klinten, Klintevej 8, 8305 Ballen, tel: 86 59 20 44 – hostel in a former hotel, right on the beach with 23 family rooms.

Index